STAR FIRE
DISCLOSURE
UPDATED

SPECIAL EDITION RARE PHOTOS

STORY BY ANNA STARFIRE. TEXT BY L.L. GRANGER

Dedicated to Rita, Buzzy, Susan, Anne, Shane, Arthur, Bingo, Dion and Mr. S. You were so brave and you are so dead from the RFID cancer chip and the car accidents. I promised you everyday of my life I would try to tell somebody, anybody. Nobody listened and nobody cared.

To my little ones in small worlds....You ARE so brave. Our words don't work anymore but action does. Eyes wide open now; Be Brave. I will come back with much bigger beams next time. Someday somebody will pay a price for the Sins of the Fathers. It WON't be me next time.

Table of Contents

#1 Secret Space Program

I am sending a story you may or may not find interesting or believable. Either way as a human being and vaccine chimera, I feel it is my duty to at least alert you to the possibility my story could be true.

I received my RFID chip a long time ago during illegal experiments in military labs. I was a brain injured orphan and subjected to transplants, vaccines and surgeries. I make these claims because I was donated to science labs for MK Ultra experiments in 1961-1975. I received cell transplants into my optical lobes from insect species and other donors. The doctors inserted very long hollow needles up my nose containing the tiny geode cells of insects and birds. I was a little girl and very lucky to survive at all. I can prove some claims.

This book has photographs of me, a 15 month old baby wearing a metal halo implant used for GPS experiments. I have photos which show the outlines of other metal implants using a serial port style plug. These objects were actually imbedded into my growing brain. I can show the surgical scars and what appears to be a missing cornea from fifty year old photos with Kodak time stamps. That's what I got.

I am an MK Ultra survivor used in different experiments for brain, body and technology interface and implants. I was implanted with metal objects, electronic sensors, optic light rays and experimental brain cells. My medical records are in classified files from still secret MK Ultra Projects. My project experiments dealt with mind control, beam weapons, child sex, pharmacology and new psychology. Most of the experiments were cruel and illegal so I can't get my records.

I am still a mini radio tower all by myself thanks to left over equipment and crystal implants in my holographic brain. I am semi-classified now so I can talk about disclosure and the experiments from MK Ultra labs. My efforts are focused on bringing attention to civil rights issues concerning extreme uses for technology like brain implants, satellite based ABA tones, hypnosis, emotional stimulation platforms and other techniques to develop our identity.

I am concerned that mind control weapons are injuring our brains and causing autism, mental illness, obsessions and so forth. I know that cells were grown for chimera implants and used in vaccines on experimental children. I have solid reasons for suspecting that this is the case of our secret shadow government.

I feel it is urgent for science to disclose the existence of other advanced species. I want science and the labs to explain what they put in us; as vaccines, shots and crystals. The ingredients put in vaccines are not always nice and may contain genetic time bombs for dates of extinction at a personal and bloodline level.

MK Ultra, Florida, Space & Technology

The MK Ultra projects had far reaching scope and future impact on technological development including the space program. Even fifty years ago, various agenda driven and privately funded groups of scientists were working on genetics to create human-hybrid species and advanced warriors like super soldiers. Their mind control programs were linked to vaccine development because tiny RFID chips were synched to satellites and cell towers. Vaccines gave us the reason to get the shot and secret chip.

The MK Ultra projects were funded to use mind control for a better population. As such, the scientists used children in State care programs for technology experiments. The State planners also allowed the use of disabled people for experiments into robotics. Many hundreds of Florida's disabled children and adults died in absolutely inhumane and cruel experiments. The folks with autism were highly prized because most could walk and had good loco-motor skills. Hundreds of disabled residents just disappeared. Dear reader, the people with autism just disappeared. Even worse, non-disabled children playing in the street just disappeared and their families never heard from them again.

Shadow Government

When the growth of the nation was considered for the post WWII year spans, the planners and leaders were faced with running two governments. The first was public and positive with open laws and hearings. Justice was possible. It was composed of new families, immigrants and exciting possibility for change and growth. We the people could make a good life if we tried.

The second was the world-wide Shadow government and it planned all the angles of the fifty year watch. It had to deal with the reality of life with people. The military and the scientists, the religions, the CIA, psychologists, senators, generals, judges and police all agreed to protect the Free Will Control Machine.

The New World Order

They called it the New World Order. They set about the invention of public structures to give us legal rights. To support the Shadow government they created legal loopholes like executive orders and state secrets. It was easy. Then the CIA directors created a system of funding for The Projects.

There was a public space program that was openly funded. There was a secret space program that was black budget funded. In those days, the space program was sold for investments. These included big names like Disney, Anheuser-Busch, Mars Candy Company, Monsanto, Cargill, Dow, McDonald and others because the parks used satellite based technology. The stockholders got fabulously rich.

These big interest groups developed the telecoms, media and entertainment which had names like Universal, National and Time. But by far, the telecoms were the most advanced in light technology. These linked to the defense industry, the educational system and politics.

Foster Care System

In the 1960's the MK Ultra labs operating in Florida developed the foster care program with CIA oversight. State law officers and adoption agencies coordinated services to the children of Florida.

State agencies were funded and developed with national dollars. The native people in Florida were terrified of the CIA agents. MK Ultra labs and experiments resulted in some native people receiving experimental surgery and psychology whether they like it or not. These included lobotomy and brain tissue harvesting for vaccine testing.

The doctors began to breed, adopt and incarcerate infants and children from native bloodlines and by genetic selection usually brain damage. This created multi-generational crime families and they needed DNA to fix their family genetic mutations. The Human CIA scientists were stealing our native species for cloning. The results were astounding.

The CIA and Other Shadow Governments developed the whole concept of aliens from the strange species that live on earth. These are not strange. They are well known and studied like birds, bees and butterflies. The makers of vaccines were interested in their parts like antennae and brain molecules.

The men even hunted our woods for Bigfoot DNA. It was a contest for swamp hunters in Florida. This was Florida's Shadow Government in the 1960's.

Swamp Chop Shops

The men that worked in Florida's secret shadow government supplied orphans and infants to scientists with the intention of creating a new hybrid species for the space program. Many hundreds of CIA agents were assigned to Florida and employed in government structures and the insurance industry.

They embedded themselves in the foundations of social programs created by President Johnson in 1965. They often worked to coordinate the services to poor and disabled people. In this manner, they were able to track, locate and identify families that produced genetic offspring with damage.

In terms of pedophiles, they simply looked for single mothers and children. They looked for poverty and abandoned people. They looked for genetic syndromes and conditions like six toes. They picked them up and put them in white vans and drove off.

They set up secret genetic testing labs in hospitals for the sick and disabled. The doctors, professors, CIA psychologists and satellite architects linked experimental medicine into the brains and bodies of Florida's most vulnerable residents. The education system was linked to the foster care system was linked to orphanages.

During the cold war era of the 1960's and 70's the CIA assigned teams of doctors and educators to learn about child development. They worked with universities in Florida, Missouri, Louisiana, Washington, D.C. and Alabama. The programs authorized by President Johnson led to the development of the foster care system.

The other piece of law that Johnson signed was a secret executive order allowing big multi-national corporations, Queens and the other advanced life forms (aka aliens) access to ALL else.

These allowed research experiments to cull children from agencies and care systems. I suspect that is why the CIA claimed all MK Ultra documents were destroyed during the Warren Commission Hearings in 1975. Does this make sense to readers?

#2 Foster Care Monarch #47

That is how I arrived in the MK Ultra program in 1962. I had a series of child abuse accidents that furthered my adventure into beam warfare, brain sculpting and vaccine programs. That is how I got into the special hospital labs and surgical suites for experimental people.

In those years, teams of MK Ultra CIA agents and doctors developed programs to identify injured infants to learn about the human brain. These moved with the person as they grew to cover the life span of the "alien" implanted individual. They were GPS tracked by satellites. Over time surgically implanted radio crystals yielded valuable information and provided hearing to the child. When the targeted children grew into adults they stayed in the secret project as test subjects.

Furthermore, some of the people used as children have no idea they have radio implants in their brains. Many of these people lived near space centers, amusement parks or military bases. That is WHY it is so important to demand our leaders explain their national security programs.

Secret technology and beam warfare can be used to hurt our minds, bodies and souls and certainly cause aggravation. For nearly fifty years I have waited for the chance to speak about my MK Ultra experiences as a survivor of experimental medicine. My lab experiments were performed in 1961 to 1974. They were part of the famous and declassified MK Ultra experiments.

Radionics Experiments on Kids

Every other summer until I was 15 years old, I had implant surgeries and brain tissue biopsies for vaccine testing and pharmacology. I was implanted with metal halos and shapes for satellite location or early GPS testing. Once I was implanted with a metal halo I travelled for satellite and radar tracking experiments. I was moved around for GPS tracking points in the states of Florida, Missouri, Arkansas, Tennessee, Kentucky, Georgia, North Carolina and Alabama.

I had many military handlers and CIA employees perform hypnosis sessions prior, during and after the surgeries and implants. It was often the way I was given to handle the pain post implant and surgery.

Sometimes when I was in a field hospital I was given dreamtime drugs to induce altered states of consciousness. I was put into experimental comas so my brain could be engineered with radio crystals and special earth species cells.

In the altered states of consciousness I could make contact with other energy fields and many were formed with consciousness from other earth species. I was very aware and intelligent when I was in the altered states.

The doctors of psychology noticed that when I woke up I had symptoms like flapping and hand wringing. I could not talk anymore because I had lost that ability. They said I was a selective mute and had amnesia. At least that is what I remember from those days. I closed my eyes and plugged my ears. I didn't want to hear the voice of them anymore or see my handlers ever again. They tortured me.

In 1966, I was diagnosed with acquired autism during my IQ test. A whole battery of child development tools were administered using school kids from counties near the Cape Kennedy Space Center. We used to be taken to a mysterious yellow trailer on old Kennedy Space Center property with a side entrance named B gate down a dirt road. Our foster parents drove us to these secret entrances and flashed their CIA badges at the guard gate.

Autism Diagnosis

Lots of the foster care kids, especially boys, ended up like me in the 1960's vaccine trials. After the shot my body changed drastically. I did not want to talk and became totally introverted. I could quietly follow directions and that was enough to survive my home life in foster care.

I knew I was different and strange. Autism was a good excuse not to talk about the extended world around me. I could feel energy, hear electricity and much more but I would not talk about it. I could figure things out about light and angles and the colors of light. I grew strong intuition rays of thought and started to study books about science, geography, societies and so forth.

I designed little experiments to study mutations using the creatures in my back yard like the tadpoles in the ditch. I told absolutely nobody. My foster family had lots of biological kids so I kept to myself. It was easy. However, over my head were spy planes and in my ears were radio crystals. My eyes took photos with the implanted fiber optics in my brain.

Eventually the doctors wanted to study me and create an IQ range and psychological categories of autism spectrum behaviors. I was trying to keep any weird body movements to myself. In those days people with autism were beaten as punishment or worse; donated for chop shop.

Brain-Body Connections in Chop Shop

Sometimes I would be installed as a plug brain to a computer. I called myself an Algobot. My neurological development was measured as electrical energy output during node development. The computer wrote behavioral stimulation algorithms as beam energy points. My whole body and brain structures were mapped using computers, electricity and acupuncture.

The brain-body connection map documented HOW the brain grew and its' pulse points. The experimenters wanted to see when neurological growth happened using the idea that quantum physics plugs energy into the rest of the body. The neuroscientists also documented the developmental time periods the energy center came online in the child's body.

The end result was a map of a brain and body that had been shot with light like folded accordion style layers of brain tissue, skin, bones, nerves and teeth. Twenty-five years later these things became advanced medical devices like the MRI machines and the CT scanners. Because I grew up on the lab computer as a brain plug I had many types of secretive men and women in my life. They were secretive so I silently followed them. I spied on them whenever I had time off from pin comb robotics or transplant surgery. I followed them and I listened. I was autistic and did not talk nor did I want to talk.

My MK Ultra style CIA lab circle contained doctors, pirates, industrialists, engineers, architects, biologists, and professors. I was a very little orphan girl of 4 or 5 years old. I had no power so I invented an alter ego that had my own name and birthday as a rank. I invented myself as a little fairy but I did not want to forget that I was a human. I used my birthday for that identity. Mr. D. knew about the fairies and he made a movie. His fairy liked nature too.

Tiny Mother Nature Spy

I decided that I would be a Mother Nature spy. I decided to spy back for the alien species like algae, moth and eel. I called it Old Mossed. It was from ancient Babylon. I promised all the transplanted species that got killed going into me for these crazy experiments that I would take us, me, myself, to college. In the meantime, I decided to pair Old Mossed with an update of information that I called String Theory.

String theory was a big component of space warfare planning using particle beams, laser beam cannons and space beam weapons. I figured out that the beams of light that are so healing in radionics arrangements were going to be used to make war on people. It was going to allow criminals to have fine lives. I could hardly stand it. I prayed to Jesus and so I invented my own way to handle the light wars of archangels.

By the age of 6, I invented my own my prayer based string theory. I called it the way of natural light and natural life. It was the opposite of the artificial beam program. My string theory could be activated with prayers through the name of Jesus.

I wanted species to know him so we would have a spiritual way to proceed with the many years ahead that I had to face. I needed an Archetype of Unconditional Love and to me that was Jesus. I needed a style of religion that could allow for all the little ones inside of me to be loved too. No earth priests allowed. Absolutely, no CIA was allowed in my club because demons do not change. I hated them with a wicked force because every single one of them sexually abused children. Every single one of them. Period.

Only true species like bees, butterflies, minnows, little kittens, trees and so forth could be in my club. I held it as my alter ego. I was a wonderful fairy in that world, not the brain damaged orphan with autism.

I was the new kid self-elected leader of Old Mossed group representing the interests of Mother Nature. I was going to love all the species that I got vaccinated with and learn about them in school.

Looking back in time, I see how I tried to survive physical & mental cruelty and make the best of it. I tried to find a way to respect the hybrid creature I was.

#3 Genetic Groupies

My ideas for Old Mossed came from watching Mr. D. and Golda M. in the early 1960's robotic experiments. It was when they created the technical color studio in Orlando. The two of them worked together on the physics of light and sounds. They had books with the math equations of Mr. Einstein from Germany.

I believe they may have made a hologram of Einstein, Tesla, the Roosevelts and other genius people and linked it to a huge cray super computer. I thought maybe I was crazy to think this stuff but there is an actual Hall that the elite group made into an amusement park exhibit. The Hall features talking robots who tell their history as talking political robots.

By the early 1960's the amusement park companies, political families and governments had their brand new labs above ground and underground. They were creating the future right out in the open in front of everyone using the latest and greatest technology. They built different types of theme parks like sea, river, technology, culture and so forth.

They were so advanced and creative that I thought they were grey alien-human-bee hybrid people so I decided to spy on them. They took special shots to help them and plugged into computers like me. Looking back, the special shots were probably something to make altered states like opium or relieve cancer pain like Mr. D. had. When I was a kid in lab experiments I saw them do it on make shift hospital lab tables in Orlando. They were rats and plugs too.

Radiation Damage Mutates Genetics

During MK Ultra projects, I participated in experiments using the cells from different species to correct a problem due to radiation damage to our DNA. I received vaccines with butterfly bits and algae pieces.

The CIA doctors said they had to do implants and it had to do with the light of the sun and radiation. The biologists studied different types of insect species looking for useful parts. Butterflies, moths and insects have soft DNA. Algae collects white light ions and interacts with photons.

The insect DNA is very responsive to toxins and radiation. That is WHY I was put in a 50 year study whether I liked it or not.

Fish Eggs Develop Reptile Brains

The scientists in most of the different genetic labs had figured out that the reptilian portions of our brains are connected to a much bigger brain. That is because in fetal development of most of earth's species, our life forms pass through the fish stage, egg stage and reptile stage on the way to becoming human. Think about it. Cats, dogs, lizards, birds and all kinds of life SHARE these forms. It gets a little touchy for the designers of life to watch it destroyed or mutated beyond recognition.

The scientists called the fish to egg to reptilian brain a unified field of consciousness. They decided to try many different types of experiments on the developmental cycle. They used the reptilian brain; both big and small sizes. The elite groups brought their pharmaceutical drugs and the space group brought their beam telemetry codes.

The reptilian brain and the egg it came from were targeted for change. In humans, the reptilian brain could be sectioned away from other structures and more easily defined. The elite had lots of new chemicals and plastics they wanted to test. They were going to need lots and lots of brains in all kinds of sizes.

The alligator brain could replace the "human man" so they would not have to donate. Instead the CIA designed another Swamp Hunter Contest during the late 1960's. I saw swamp hunters grab big alligators and cut their brains out and put them in coolers for transplant into kids. I was very upset to see the necks of kids with stitches and grey brain implants. What in the world were they doing with surgical implants and radio crystals?

Aliens Synch Assist Light Code

There were extraterrestrial groups that wanted to assist synching the reptilian brain with any new light code in our collective environments. The process of light synching with DNA was invaded by certain criminal elements and cosmic predators. They were interested in collecting human DNA. This was the big deal for secrecy. The extraterrestrial groups and human agenda groups wanted to manipulate the body, brain and soul (fish-sperm-ova-egg) of human beings.

Food Additives for Beams

The doctors and shadow groups chose to use insect parts like antennae that could embed in the brains of young children and not be rejected by the body. The antennae attracted colored dyes and were used as markers in the brain. When the doctors physically opened the brain they could photograph or use sketch artists to depict the dye locations on the brain. In this manner, the scientists could actually match sight of lesion in the upper brain or motor cortex to a similar region on the reptilian brain. This affected the whole spinal column and brain development.

Vaccine Ingredient Testing

Once the brain polyp was ready it could be surgically removed and it was already marked by a color code of dye stain. Often the polyps removed were grown with special ingredients like metals or magnetic Nano particles. These magnetic Nano particles could be added to food very easily. They are the same particles in your credit card magnetic strip only in particle form. So just touching public surfaces will add some magnetic Nano particles to skin and blood. These vibrate in the presence of microwave beams especially infrared ones.

#4 Personal Testimony

On a personal level, the scientists designed satellites with mind control beams to match the RFID chips implanted in my brain. They created different brain areas as targets for their microwave beams by using colorful food dyes. I endured shots directly into my motor cortex and brain stem containing food dyes. I cried and was miserable after I woke up from the swelling and coma the shots would cause me. It would take three to six months to heal my walking and talking.

After my brain would heal, I would go back to live with the CIA foster family. My sponsor parents would make me go outside and sit on the grass while they taught me about the new jet contrails. My father showed me the difference between water vapor and chemicals. They said that the world leaders were going to spray the Nano bots on people to control them. They would be on almost every single plane someday.

It took the scientists and the CIA engineers a few troublesome years to perfect their mind control programs and weather wars. The navy would fly their geoengineering planes and create a chemical contrail. Usually within a few minutes I would hear a tone. Sometimes I saw orb shaped bright lights in the sky. Sometimes after they did all this I would find myself standing naked and bleeding in my bathroom. There was no 911 to call in those days. I was on my own.

I believe that once the CIA and corporations got the technology worked out they went crazy. They used pencil beam rays and sunshine canons to fire laser beams at people, animals and trees. They found minerals like gold under private property too. They used words like bull's eye, target and lock. The made a law called Eminent Domain for the government of the elite to use so they could reclaim property from past wars. At least that is what they told me; a young Mother Nature spy at the time.

Selective Mute on the Spectrum

I was a selective mute after the experiments for vaccines and satellite radio tracking. I had lots of trauma from the experiments and the CIA handlers. I had many operations.

In one of the most profound, I was surgically implanted with dyes and teeny tiny holographic projector crystals. I was held for surgery at Sunland Hospital during its preopening phase in the mid 1960's. The doctor used very long forceps to insert the crystals behind my eardrum. My ears were still growing because I was only 4 years old. I was also injected with dyes during open brain surgery. After I was released from the hospital to go to my sponsor home I felt very sick as if exposed to radiation and chemo therapy.

Holographic Human Minds

In the 1970's and 80's the introduction of radio crystals for human mind control was done on the population at large. The brain scientists and computer technicians know that the human brain is a projector of reality. It is dependent on all the mass projectors or human mind crystals generating a regional picture of a spot in space and time or holographic matrix. Our brains filter this type of white light into a hologram of colorful ions we perceive as sight and optical recognition patterns. We humans take it for granted that we have colorful sight. Other species are not so lucky.

The reader has to consider the military as the biggest supporter of biological research and vaccines. This story has not even bothered to name the old government agencies who used to protect us like the Federal Communication System or the Food Protection Agency. They are corrupt and sold human beings out a very long time ago. Now it's just a contest on who can survive the extremes of psychological manipulation and torture. This is Pluto; the planet of secrets and psychology and strange food crystals to eat and drink.

Alien Light Technology

The aliens could synch up with machines using holographic beams to fly their craft. The Militaries of the World wanted to have the same technology. It was called light code by the aliens and it worked wherever there was light.

The alien species could synch their body systems to their flying space craft. They military wanted a new brain for programming so they could fly similar ships at the same speed of light the aliens used. All of the research labs in the world were struggling to develop light technology like lasers and fiber optics. Once they were successful a host of products and military missions could begin.

Optical Laser Surgery

This technology was being used to perform laser surgery nearly fifty years ago before lasers were officially invented. I have photographic evidence to suggest that corneal transplants were performed by high tech laser surgery in 1961. Even then high technology was being hidden from the general public.

The doctors in my state were given orphans and good equipment to develop human potentials. Within two or three months of my birth in 1961, doctors performed open brain surgery to create artificial tracks of living proteins from spider silk and prion strings of fibers. The goal was to create new optical, visual and motor tracks once the lobotomy had scraped a trail clear of original cells. My original cells were replaced with species cells with soft DNA codes.

They performed the special implantation surgery to sculpt my brain over a span of 11 years. These are some of the pictures from my personal collection of surgical scars. I was used to craft another species; a new and improved species of human origin and probably some that are not.

1961 Photo: Infant Brain Sculpting Scars

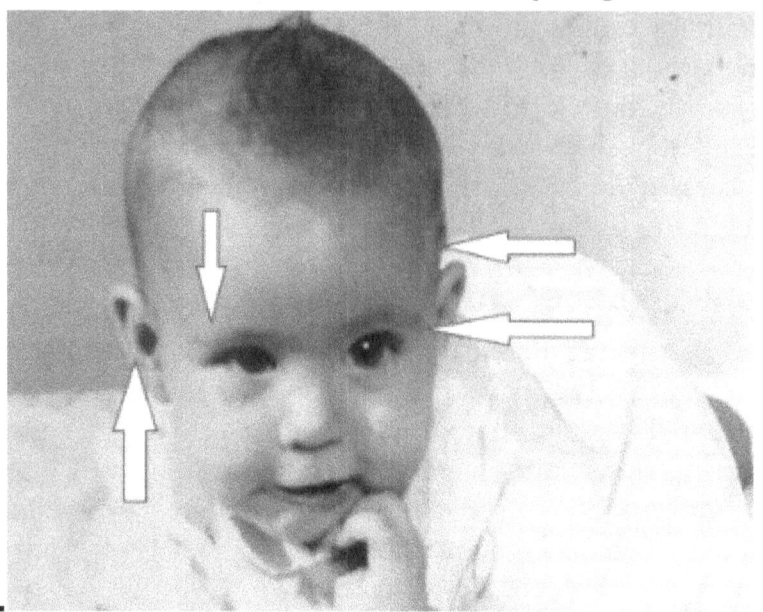

The down arrow to the eyebrow area shows where the optic nerve was opened behind the eyeball. The double arrows near the ears point to the implant surgery to deposit radio crystals. The cornea is missing from the right eye.

Secret Surgery with Lasers

I was initially adopted through a branch of Catholic charities involved with strange genetic experiments. I may have been a donor child to a secret project the Queen of England developed to hybridize particular species into human beings. Other specie cells were gifted to me in later implants.

The location of my birth and creation were kept secret from me because of my foster care CIA parents. They were from a multi-generational group of families associated with polygamy and extraterrestrial life.

My family members in the CIA were super smart and some were recruited from the old guard polygamists. They said they liked the idea of communism and genetic engineering. They set about creating the social systems, the welfare system, the caste system and racial inheritance. My foster family were small time players with no name last names, but they knew something about computer programming, nuclear energy and geoengineering.

#5 Geoengineering Nature

These particular shadow groups had a focus on geoengineering and energy way stations across America. They planned out highways, waterways, sanitation and military manufacturing. All of these were going to be brand new and could be engineered for now and later.

Cell towers that were linked to satellites could keep a population or an individual under control; mind control. Technology would be fed to secret groups like the CIA, FBI, NASA, MI5, etc. from both Space Coasts. To improve the use of beam telemetry and mind control the military built secret bases in California (Area 51) and Florida (Cape Kennedy). It all made sense. To secretly celebrate their achievements', they built the unusual St. Louis Arch. It one of the first GPS points photographed from space.

The very first computer programmers and satellite designers were based in St. Louis, Missouri. Many had come to America with doctorate degrees from German, French and Persian universities. They were associated with prestigious universities in the Midwestern states of Arkansas, Missouri and Illinois. They had connections into Mexico, California and Nevada because of gold and silver. They also had long histories of slavery and polygamy.

These co-dependent male connections grew over time into organized political parties and family interdependency. These were secretly connected to the military through the CIA and similar shadow government organizations. They are naturally attracted to covert intelligence gathering because they like secrets and they like to watch us do very private things.

The Hunt for the Arks

These groups chose St. Louis based on a number of factors having to do with the extraterrestrial issue. There has been some discussion that the exact location of Noah's Ark was placed incorrectly in Iran. The word Ozark sounds a lot like Noah's Ark doesn't it? Maybe the place of the Ark was in the mountains of Ozark. If so, the CIA figured that someone would come and find it. The hunt for extraterrestrial life began in both Missouri and Arkansas. The Missouri groups did not want the Arkansas groups to find the Ark and the hidden technology mentioned in Babylonian records.

The CIA sent agents into large employment centers like the telephone companies. They would run a story of ET invasion and listen into the conversations and stories. Those kinds of counter-intelligence operations brought out lots of stories of sightings of both craft and creatures. Artifacts started to show up and bits of broken fiber optics. Eventually the CIA traced it back to some caves and a whole hidden network of underground tunnels.

Military finds ET Tunnels

It is my belief at that point the military and the secret spies from the CIA were able to start negotiating with three other races of co-dependent species including one I called the cold ground reptilians. In fact, the CIA planned a series of underground labs to network into the alien hive and tunnel system. Sometimes they would locate the end of a hive tunnel and up above would be a Church.

Churches are the places for rituals of many kinds. That is why they were important to these creatures. They knew people would come there every Sunday to pray. They knew people would baptize their babies on Saturday. It was the days of the week that made orphans.

That is HOW the two things were affiliated, the tunnels and the Churches and especially the Mosques. That is WHY experiments into genetics happened with no oversight on the poor orphans left behind.

The secret government set up their very real above ground operations that supported their own top secret research and development labs. They called these places Zoos. They elite investors and CIA operate these types of secret genetic labs out in the open and can match most of the alien DNA found to earth species. That is how they started to figure out the roots of WHO the aliens really were.

Recombinant Genetics

When the CIA studied the aliens they figured out their connections on the genetic level to human beings and to human DNA strands. They decided to experiment on DNA and add lost genetic strands. They called this junk DNA and told us not to worry about it. Instead, their secret labs looked at ways to give those bits more energy and to possible reassemble those bits for links to higher technology including mind control.

I was surgically altered for technology and implanted with radio crystal implants. My surgeries gifted the cells of species to the optic and acoustic nerves. Somebody was using advanced lasers in secret underground labs to remove infant corneas.

The surgery may have created a new optical chasm for fiber optic implants into my living, growing and thinking brain. Were these the first optical scanners ever invented? In later experimental surgeries as I grew up, my brain was implanted and sculpted with living cells taken from species to add more holographic dimensions to my experience. Obviously, some of these experiments were designed to develop the color photocells in human brains that synched with the brains of other species. It also created a technological marvel at the time the optical holographic brain scanner and data retrieval system. Me.

Synch Brains to Radiation Levels

Fifty years ago these experiments began as honest attempts to repair damage from nuclear weapon testing in the upper atmosphere. It was a quantum idea to try and repair broken DNA. Our world is probably more colorful than 50 years ago. We may even find ways to keep our sun healthy since our science and now our genetics are based on species experience and human interventions. However, in those days it was urgent and human beings were mutating at midline. More children were being born with birth defects than ever before. The damage was obvious.

Small World to the Rescue

The small world of insects has at least 10,000 years of species evolution on earth. This is important because they captured a record of our sun's ions and beams. They evolved photon collection systems and evolved with the sun and nuclear energy present on earth. The reptilian species has an even older history in the universe. In order to attempt to repair the human genome and possible improve it, secret experiments took place.

In my X-man theory, the photo cells of the donor species wrapped around the brain tracks of metals and protein. When data beams were pointed from satellites the tracks grew as an optional data source in my baby brain. My visual cortex got used to accepting the data code.

I grew what I think was an optical scanner for reading light codes and alphabets. That is one of the reasons that I think my brain was modified. I believe these species cells transmitted data to and from new points on the human body. The brain mapping was done using electrified field theory to achieve quantum states with solid state acupuncture needles.

#6 Brain Was Mapped

The idea that Artificial Intelligence (A.I.) would look for its own history using frequency and sonar is one of importance to the Archetype of Consciousness.

Once this idea of artificial intelligence looking for itself was accepted, the notion of looking for similar energy signatures was developed. Shortly after that, the familiar flat chip circuits was reinvented for brain implants. Once a suitable area was discovered in the auditory processing center the brain implants of tiny squares could be photographically and chemically etched in the brain tissue for data retrieval and projections. The Universes held in the holograms could be decoded in a space/time field. They were held in suspended animation called a light pane. These little chip cards could potentially yield the location of ancient computers and space processors if they were planted in growing brains. They could yield a timeline for time travel and "repairs" to the timeline by the elite.

The Job of Implants

The implants might "Wake Up" if they were in the same type of energy field the original A.I. was born in. They did and they do. When HAARP weapons pass over the old cores and tech equipment they make sounds like a deep vibrating string.

A RFID chip can be stimulated by HAARP codes and create physical sensations. When the light codes are stimulated by HAARP at the same resonant frequencies, the human implant person has memories and possible physical pain. Humans have symptoms associated with psychic phenomena and animals sometimes act strangely or howl. HAARP is not always a bad thing. These sounds can gather the radio waves into slower rhythms so they can harmonize better. Nature gets greener and spring can bloom.

Bioluminescence and Smell Molecules

The deep brain was connected to the outside world by molecules of odor and the sense called smell. The molecular nature of smell was tied to light and something else called bioluminescence. Scientists found out that smells and bioluminescence were highly addicting and created lots of pleasure and feelings.

Bioluminescence could be released by species as a unified field of light, sounds and smells that was a show of subtle agreement and harmony. When that happened, light beams caused the release of highly charged molecules and the season called spring could invent itself. Bioluminescence was a species protected agreement. So were grain codes and general happiness at having eyes to see our Sun.

Bioluminescence had quantum resonance features identified as a physics bridge and linked to structures in the deep brain. The bioluminescent ability of human beings was most apparent in the meninges of their brain. The meninges captured ions and filtered them to the pineal glands of males and adrenal glands of females. The American Indians created the dream catchers as a tool to remember ions are released back into light. This happens at night too during dream cycles that should not be there.

The hard palate had special cells that could decode the different molecules and taste them too. Apparently these were really old body structures that had lost some of their functional ability. These areas on the body with special cells were studied like cellular gear an astronaut body would need to receive information from far away. For instance, if a human astronaut living on a new planet wanted to see if a leaf was edible he'd need to just touch a tiny bit to his palate and ask the computer to analyze it.

The science called anthropology and sociology went even further into the past and surmised that these computers had existed before, but how? And more importantly, where? It was growing obvious that humans had advanced computers and beam telemetry in the past.

Designing a Grey Alien

Mr. D's group had plans to build secret underground labs based at his amusement parks in Florida and California for growing clones. He let big companies help plan the attractions for display and experiment for the future. He used technology and sponsored research on improving food, nutrition and genetic control of seed production. All of his experiments were linked into other projects like the GMO foods served at all his park sites. The royal amusement park group was highly successful at developing the technology we have today such as the robotics, holograms, optical scanners, retinal readers and barcoded footprints. All of this individual data was linked to underground computers and robotics. Some was actually shot out to space and recorded on computers in captured telemetry beams.

Long Term Planning

Over the next 20 years, Mr. D. and his royal amusement park groupies planned attractions in Japan and France. I think they wanted secret programs with cloned grey aliens to run interference, blame and guard the elite. The plans for a new grey alien species included the specially grown sectional brain that could be implanted as a suitable brain. It was to be placed in a durable caterpillar like body. The plan was humanoid with 2 legs and 5 fingers.

These were part of Mr. D.'s original plans for cloning grey aliens. The actual plastic molds were seeded with various growth hormones and located in Japan. The body was grown from a large silk worm type of material with silicon lacing structures for data based alien neurology. The grey aliens were designed to consume hydrogen products using freeze dried crystals provided by earth pharmaceutical labs.

The plans for clones were long in place. The military and secret elite families, used alien bodies after capture from crashes like Roswell 1947. Those bodies were scavenged for implantable tissue or technology like the brain chips.

These experimental species with A.I. implants, would secretly become a new family attached to an old species with upgraded genetics and resistant strains. In order to make the demo grey aliens, the scientists used different combinations. In all honesty, the experiments were using mixed genetics with some base line ancestors like the bee. They used others and I followed the collection as I was synched up. I call the varieties of grey alien life forms the mariposa greys, the rana or frog type greys and my favorites, the cat greys. According to the secret space military and the secret CIA, the addition of these new experimental animals-hybrids-humans with A.I. would occur whether anyone like it or not.

#7 Treaty Aliens

Frogs, butterflies and bees are easy to find, but human-hybrids are not and real live aliens are even harder. The genetics of the alien species got purer and purer until they had fixed the genetic problem. I saw one of the tall grey of bee species at the secret Graham airfield lab in 1972. She turned and took one long, look at me and I took a long, look back.

I was on the plug computer in a hospital bed set up at the airfield in the old administration building. I could see the runway out of the window. I was not going anywhere. Directly above the runway at 10,000 feet in the air was a ship with a small crew of greys. The ship had advanced telemetry and GPS with at least one Mr. D. style holographic projector. The tall grey alien was able to make an appearance at the make-shift hospital by beaming down from the ship.

Apparently, the tall grey alien was checking on the kids that had been surgically deposited with the species cells. They kept orphans and runaways for experiments at the nearby Sunland hospital.

Since I was working for the Old Mossed team and representing Mother Nature I decided to spy. Please understand that I did like the people from Israel. The Old Mossed is from ancient India with origination in ancient Babylon during the first reign of Kings and Queens.

I realized I could encrypt what was happening as a similar program the computer would accept by calling it Old Mossed from Babylon. I could verify the Babylonia connections to these families through the A.I. computer. I could ask it questions and get the answers. I sent my own super data set of impressions and memories back through the plug in my head. My data ran back to a super cray computer that was collecting childhood growth data for a BIOS developmental program I worked on. It had crossing points in Babylon for genetics, alien interventions, nuclear wars and the development of language for society.

That means much of the light codes from Babylon matched the story of the Anunnaki. The humans knew without a doubt that human-alien-hybrids and intelligent design were real. When the crossing points of humans and aliens became too obvious the contact between the aliens in space and the CIA happened at Graham air field. This is what I observed in my field of operations.

The MK Ultra CIA scientists were running around with clipboards. Everyone looked scared. There were some important royal families, including the Saudi Kings that came to meet the tall grey. The scientists had checklists and vials of proteins. It was space trade too and they had found a Babylonian ancestor of immense power.

Space Trade: Slaves, Drugs & Metals

I found out that in the case of grey aliens one of their objectives was to see in high definition light fields with colorful sight receptors. They had damaged eye shield lenses and needed transplant lenses. They had corresponding damage to their special auditory structures on their brain stems from radiation and detonation flashes. Light damaged their hearing systems.

In the secret experiments to help synch assist the greys, some of the donor kids had butterfly sight molecules implanted in their cerebellums. After the cerebellum grew the special cells for the transplant experiments some of the kids were killed and burned in Sunland ovens. I thought I was a going to be burned up too after they all left Graham airfield and the makeshift hospital labs.

Vaccines linked to Weather War Beams

In 1960's there were extensive space coast experiments to link Heaven to Earth. The scientists chose the grey brain stem to create a space program linking vaccines to satellites and cell tower warfare. That is why our vaccines parts are color coded. The colors draw rays and beams to specific brain structures during infancy and childhood.

Our ears have natural crystals and some artificial crystals. Some are grown with us as infants and they assist our balance for walking. When they are targeted by electromagnetic fields using even small beams, the person will get psychologically sick and behave erratically with emotional outbursts. All of that can be caused by beams.

Working Theory of Clusters

I grew up to be a researcher and scientist but I could never remember the MK Ultra experiments. My mind had blocked them for obvious reasons. In any case, I found myself compelled to study autism and cancer. So much of my life had been spent dealing with those two conditions. I decided to see if I could write a spectrum theory to explain clusters of autism and cancers. I subconsciously began to bring my own knowledge into the present time.

I brought beams and ray stimulation into my working theory of autism. I decided to include beam stimulation with the idea of species RNA from vaccines being responsive to light. The behaviors might become expressed and exaggerated by beam weapons and cause autism clusters or similar cancer clusters. This was the ONLY way I could explain clusters of disorders.

I had to consider satellites and massive beam warfare on neighborhoods. The military and the police have microwave beam weapons on cell towers, radio equipment, drones, blimps and satellites. Obviously, microwave beams are common and can be very dangerous. Certain wavelengths of microwaves can cause severe symptoms because they go into tissue rather deeply.

Molecular Lesions from Bee Molecules

During the vaccines experiments in Florida, holographic crystals were taken from species. One of the cell types for vaccine replication was collected from the head of a bee for sight. The species of bee had a vibrational rate assigned on a satellite and all of the bee cells in the targeted area vibrate to the beam when it passed over the street, neighborhood or city.

The vibration caused a teeny tiny lesion but it was enough blood to allow a spot link. The vaccine codes caused heavy metals and magnetic particles to accumulate in know areas of the brain like the cones of the eyes. The weapon designers engineered a blood spot link with beams and A.I. by causing a tiny brain lesion. Remember that sand jumps (bee molecules) in a base sound field and so does teeny tiny magnetic pieces of metals.

Later the scraping beams got bigger and more accurate. The poor little brain that I saw in pictures looked scraped up with tiny bloody pin holes when these types of energy weapons were used.

My theory suggests that beams be considered has contributing factors towards autism and ADHD type behaviors not to mention mental illness. These should be ruled out as external causes in an honest diagnosis. Our big organizations like the Medical Association should be held accountable for missing these external factors in the diagnosis of mental and physical disorders.

Beams can be are common enough and constant enough to potentially form gas from water in our bodies. This might get hot enough around the spot lesions to cook the brain tissue in minute pin prick holes. The microwaves might be given as a pulsed energy field by military fly overs from satellite surveillance teams. Most at risk would be the developing fetus, newborns and vaccine recipients. The areas around the optic and acoustic nerves were often targeted by weapons designers.

Redundant Systems

A safe light spectrum in the environment is very important to human development. Injury to a fetus or a newborn might cause a redundant system in the reptilian brain to take over normal functions like walking or talking. As the child grew up and got even more synch crystals and vaccines, the chances of severe autism increased dramatically. The higher learning of the white matter brain would be damaged and the resulting behaviors would be odd. They would fit symptoms of autism psychology like flapping, rocking and moaning.

Microwaves also cook eggs and sperm and this is part of population control. Radiation comes along with microwave beams and plasma screens. There are other rays from the sun like green gamma or gamma beta from cell phones, satellites and smart homes.

To a certain extent, light particles and ions are expected to travel through a light body with no ill effects. Cities are very densely lit with many kinds of artificial lights which cause brain overload especially in the hearing system. Light is generated by electricity. It's in the subliminal ranges of perception.

That is HOW the hearing system can be damaged by light and its carrier electricity. That is how a human brain can be linked into the energy field of the sun or the sun of man if you are a religious reader. That is a good thing as long as the damaging rays like radiation like sun UV radiation stays out of the human body.

Satellite Phone Tag

We have been gathered together for light spectrum control and reprogramming. They are using the light beams to support society and control data flows. Our human bodies are tough but can be injured or disabled from use of the microwave light spectrum without regard for the humans. The psychologists, neurologists and beam programmers who work for the government know how the programs for beam wars work. The people should ask.

Once a person is tagged by a satellite as a test subject; they are monitored by intelligence agencies and corporate sponsors. This was so their behaviors, buying habits and decision making skills. They could be altered without the victim knowing. In some of the experiments with foster care victims, there was a radio crystal put behind the eardrum to irritate a lesion from vaccine testing. This is what happened to me; a survivor.

The vaccine holographic cells were developed to foster more unified styles of learning. The use of unified codes for light is important for all the lifeforms on a planet. In some cases people who got special vaccines in regional experiments can actually have more range of light detection.

On the psycho-emotional end of the spectrum they were so smart they pointed beams on our heads and spine to attract brain waves. Once attached to a source, the satellite could offer technical support like microwave long waves for mind control operations.

#8 Geoengineering New Pole

We know the human DNA and body must change to match the energy of a planet. During the 20th century, science allowed the unbridled use of nuclear energy in bomb explosions and core releases. Above ground detonations of nuclear radiation damages the sun and eventually shortens the life of that sun.

When the sun is damaged, our earth's magnetic alignments and poles weaken. These let loose bands of lights or ions. During the post 911 years, it appears our sun has been shielded as it appears to be installing a new halo. These bands can be unstable and affect technology like cell tower signals. Once bands leave an area they may not return to link with that geomagnetic spot. This causes desert climates and eventual land shifts. Global cooling and drought are sometimes a side effect.

HAARP and Pole Control

The CIA aerospace and cyber development teams were very interested in developing knowledge about the sun. The geoengineering teams were very interested in the poles of the planet. This was essential for weather control.

To control the people with the HAARP machines they had to coordinate with the vaccine makers. The vaccine program was able to artificially link vaccinated people into the HAARP beam fields. Once linked up to coordinates, the system could project the perception of gravity to the brains of target people. These were the GPS victims used for experiments.

The secret and public government joined to build HAARP. Eventually the HAARP system would limit the humans in order to explore the human mind. The reptilian brain was always a target for making a secret energy called cold fusion from brain wave metadata. Go look at the labels on smart homes and computer appliances. They have a blue star. This is the secret way to harvest blue beam metadata as free energy. The corporate elite and the Master type grey alien-hybrid race of beings wanted us as human test subjects so they could reboot their technology and relive the glory days of Egypt. They like slave, war and sex trafficking. We never arrest them due to the alien threat.

The Politics of Light Code Energy

Certain factions of the tall greys support their war monger humans because they are politicians by a bloodline. The alien groups who front for human agenda groups control nuclear energy from behind the scenes.

The HOW was created by media and psychologists. They used fear and secrets to do it and used the royal blood. They used the blood of Jesus to psychologically bless certain bloodlines from Babylon. This mind control tactic has allowed a mass approval of torture and genocide. All of this is with public approval.

Jesus was tortured and hung on a cross as an example. Guess who tortured him? Other Jews and Roman politicians, that's who. I believe apostles like Paul and Judas, sold him out to officials as a slave and a stooge.

What the people witnessed was the death of an activist and journalist named Jesus of Nazareth. He was tortured and hung on a cross as an example to others to keep your mouth shut and pray. Psychologically speaking; it must have been so traumatic that people wrote and saved the Bible. They wanted to tell you something so you can save your future.

The humans and other politicians got to own the nuclear power industry because the alternative media used aliens as a secret psychological tool. This is how the aliens actually gave human corporate owners power. The reality is the aliens did not do a thing on a massive social level. We did.

As far as I surmise, most of the aliens are here for a variety of reasons. They do not come here to own oil wells, scare people or steal cows. However, there are some very dangerous aliens and human-hybrid combinations that should be disclosed. It is possible they are very sick and dangerous. They use humans to represent their interests. Their politician human rep is pretty sick too. We can tell. We are under full blown mind control weapons every single day in the city.

Each of the 50 States has developed the technology they can use. Most of it defends the politicians and bankers. I wonder if this is what the alien ancestors intended to give us.

The owners of pharmaceutical labs also own the satellites and run the elite clubs. They can offer their friends technology using vaccine light codes and beam warfare to negotiate. They all protect the drugs and money flows because they have to.

Broken Rainbows

In return for the stress, the politicians and corporate kings get a fleet of black vehicles, multi-racial children and countless other human subjects for experimentation. When the sky is sick it is rare to see a completely arched rainbow with full color spectrum. The new broken rainbow means more mutations and spectrum disorders. It's happening again just like fifty year ago.

The secret space wars broke the light bows and organization of the light spectrum. I suspect that the geoengineering teams of secret societies went to work using the old light codes stored in our vaccinated brains from vaccine cell parts of moth, butterfly and algae. This is what the humans used in unwitting geoengineering projects are doing for the secret government.

Story of Autism and Light Spectrums

In my theories of what happened in MK Ultra labs, I think the electroshock therapy approach to brain sculpting produced a negative image or flipped polarity projection of brain structures and functions. The scientists used to put us under a big round ring that made a sound and pulsed energy at us; cold energy. It may have been a way to confuse the reptilian neural pathways. It might cause a bipolar disorder if the reptilian brain's function competes with the white brain's motor cortex and primary visual system.

In a redundant system, the neural pathways might overlap. The acoustic nerve may absorb light with beam stimulation. In certain tolerated frequencies this can become overwhelming to the brain. This is the wrong job for the eyes to do. This data belonged to the hearing system of a human in the frequencies instead of targeted by electromagnetic smog. We have been changed to new harmonic spectrums and new light frequencies. Our brains can't always keep up.

The visual system of rods and sight cones may absorb sound. The cones at the back of the eye could collect base and alto sound waves like a big speaker system. The function of the rods and cones in the eye may get changed forcibly from vaccines.

If the rods are coated with magnetic dust the eyeballs would hurt when exposed to light. Obviously the higher brain in charge of processing the ions from the cones might not expect sound to replace light ions.

This might cause the eyeball to bounce in the socket and produce odd behaviors. Odd behaviors can be considered as part of a polarity flip symptom. Why? Because the increased light stimulation and collection of magnetic pieces and other molecules makes the cone bulge and some explode. Sometimes seizures are triggered because of light and sound escaping the optic chasm and the eyeball. This is consistent with the diagnosis of autism and other neurological conditions.

What if the brain area is targeted with geomagnetic rays that are supported by metadata targeting? What if the rays were so strong in magnetic field strength that crystals lined up in columns along behavioral and informational data points? This might account for behaviors that include lining up toys or even some obsessive behaviors; like spinning in circles.

Many species with geo sensors like birds, bees and fish contributed to the vaccine implants and crystal harvesting of Florida. We are an interesting bunch of native mutants. The colorful photo cells and holographic crystals are a molecular miracle of our light spectrum.

Bees are a perfect example of a holographic visual system for flight and navigation. Bees use a wide variety of rays for sensory system input. Their guidance systems allow for digital and analog data bits to process through their entire little bodies. They are amazing and the scientists in my 1970's labs knew this about them.

Justice Delayed for Injured Chimeras

Back in the 1970's, the doctors and vaccine labs mass produced the butterfly DNA using digitally stained magnetic dust as a substitute. They used it on lots of children. In that case there were spinal deformities caused from the vaccine shots. Any court cases were settled out of court and there were not many that made it to the judge. Lawyers got them thrown out of court. Lawyers didn't want to handle these cases anyway because it was against something very big and powerful called the Cabal.

So far, most of the folks injured by experimental vaccines or the required injections can't get any financial or legal assistance. Sadly, most are drained dealing with the consequences of having autism, living with mental illness and all of the related issues that come from deformed spines, brains and feeling sets called emotional ranges.

Optical Telemetry Brains

One of the ways to create an optical holographic brain is to rewire it with electrical charges and metal leads. I would expect the reader to understand that this does take over the individual. There is not much defense. This is why the scientists used electroshock therapy and surgery to shape the living brain of a newborn and more recently, in Cuba and Iraq. That is why torture was used and still is on war prisoners, jail inmates, foster care orphans, etc.

The goal of the doctors and special officers was not just the gathering of information. The goal was the shaping of the gathering of information. They wanted to feed it to a specific person in a certain way. This was ultimate mind control.

People like Dr. Mengele got famous for doing it. In his case, he was a surgeon working for a large Cabal including the Royals. They invented brain surgery and even wrote a bunch of detailed plans step by step.

The medical plan was to create hollows connected by tubes and line them with the cells of species and new protein based fibers. After three months the eyes of the newborn could open and light optics could be tested.

When I was little, the crystals could receive radio wave telemetry from off world craft like satellites and human visitors. The crystals could be tuned and I could project holographic images. I could read data or documents like an optical scanner. My memory could receive the data as visual information and my auditory human brain could understand it once I got plugged into the big secret computer at Space Center. I could hear a strange high frequency to alert the military that the alien creatures were sending data transmissions. Most of the time it was feeding times and coordinates along the DMZ. Sometimes the military would use animal behavioral specialists to deal with the situation.

Somebody was sending data and using a secret human produced type of cold fusion for data. Somebody was far away like the radio bands of Jupiter. It was sophisticated spy work. I left that part of the space program when I was almost 6 years old.

#9 New Assignment

After I left the surgical and experimental MK Ultra labs, I began the most difficult part of my life in a sponsored CIA spy family. I was in foster care experiments in child sexual development. They placed children with bisexual families who tolerated child sexual abuse. The elite considered it payment to give an orphan child (slave) as a stepchild to their worker bees and employees. Not just any employees, state employees and government officials like judges or politicians.

In our State these child development projects were legitimately supported and funded as a psycho-social sexual experimental. It was part of set up of the foster care program. In order to follow children and their psychological and sexual development more closely, many children left their reform school or hospitals implanted with foreign objects.

These brain implants put into foster children were things like optical fiber implants and radio crystal implants. They were children and loaded with heavy metals and programmable chips. They could not remember what happened to them because the trauma stopped them and so did the hypnosis based mind controls. The trauma could be extreme.

Psycho-Social Sexual Disorders

I ended up with acquired autism from shots and behavioral psychology. I was actually locked in a dog caged and shocked during ABA trials. Autism IS the opposite of intimacy or trust and I think the CIA knows how it developed as a programming tool.

Autism is an acquired genetic condition based on psycho-social and sexual repression. Social repression is poverty and nobody wants to live like that. Our social responsibility was replaced with mind training and ABA hive tones. Is this the message that a vaccine synch up program sends to our brains?

If so, this is attempted murder or mass slavery for technology marvels or both. The human DNA could easily surpass the critical mark for normal reproduction and go to designer status within a very few years. Nobody wants autism, war, addiction and vaccine damaged populations. Is it okay just to program us?

Red Mercury Death

When I received a shot of red mercury in 1960's experiments I died from over exposure. I was saved with blood chelation and other emergency procedures. The metal had turned to gas and collected in my cervical spinal column. It stained most of my spinal cartilage red from the dye in the mercury vaccination.

I was angry. I had lots of repressed rage. I felt trapped in a body that hurt energetically. I could not talk to my doctors due to damage to my motor cortex and fine motor planning for speech and feeding. My foster family and military psychologists from the CIA decided to do hypnosis on me to make me somewhat functional. They had decided to use me for child sex work because I could not talk.

Even worse, my prayers were answered by satellite tones in my left ear for yes or right ear for no. I said to myself it was god on a satellite. I was not even six years old yet.

Then I was sent out to work with my CIA foster father and grandfather as a top secret infant implanted with high technology from the "alien species". They took me to meetings for monitoring. I was a project of the Jesuits and sponsored by powerful Missouri groups like the Masons.

They were talking about the future of people and how to mass control them for social planning. Sometimes I would meet with Jesuits at the university while I followed my grandfather around. They would try and comfort me by calling me an angel. I had to wear metal hoops screwed to my skull to get autism and mind controlled.

Satellite Tracking for GPS Investors

I had to wear S shapes and side rings screwed into my skull and go on hunting missions in the woods and on the beach. I could be tracked once Cape Kennedy mission control located me on the ground.

I got a unique satellite signature and beams on my mind and body. I got extensively tracked for experimental psychology and I did not know all of this as an adult. That is how powerful mind control is and the passage of time.

I think from 1961 to 1974, my personal child development of body, mind and soul was studied for the use in textbooks as general child development knowledge of the educated doctors, politicians for law making, judges, psychologists and elite military like CIA.

My sexual identity or consciousness identity was developed by psychologists from Israel, Germany, Sweden, Italy and the United States of America. My mind, body and soul training began at birth and allowed a black box of memories for satellite retrieval.

In 1964, computer programmers began to write human movements into robotic algorithms for eventual high technology use. The scientists and doctors wanted to hurry up infant and toddler sexual development. They brain mapped points for beam sculpting and nerve control. They wrote beam points on the spine for sex stimulation. They wrote beam points on the pelvis for ovulation and a management program for sperm and testes. At least that is what they called it.

By the age of 1 year old, I was satellite beam paired with sex beams to stimulate points along my spinal column. The doctors, scientists and computer satellite architects all worked together to create high technology for sexually controlled people. They could use them for watching and media like porn without them knowing.

I felt embarrassed as a kid when the controllers sent me sex stimulation beams and made my pelvis feel warm. They said I might grow up someday and want to work in the sex trade even if I was disabled by autism.

Political Satanism

When I was still an infant, I was sent to do sex work for satanic cults of politicians and priests. I was mind erased three times after three different periods of brain and body work.

Those types of experiments into the mind were done to back engineer autism. I could not talk to my doctors due to damage to my motor cortex and fine motor planning for speech and feeding. In one of the experiments the surgeons cut a piece of my tailbone off so it would be numb for pedophiles.

There were some ugly secrets under the Dome. The kids of Florida were targets. Kids with autism were desirable targets because they could not physically talk. The politicians could order them picked up and transported to reform schools; especially if the mother was single. Political egos grew unabashed.

Many people were aware of the cult aspects of intelligence agency work. Most CIA agents just got through it without saying anything to anybody. Many employees and contractors did not like the lack of honor or morality. In the active CIA dominated field of rural State politics and policies a certain superiority complex type mentality toward the native people continued in full force. Politically, the idea of Satanism as a CIA bonding ritual for scaring the agrarian based native people caught fire. Technology scared them. That is the story I know.

Politicians Hide the Truth

During the legislative sessions of the early 1960's the politicians voted every protection for the game parks and large new amusement parks. They held ritual occult killings back then in the Capitol building rotunda. The politicians and CIA agents made blood sacrifices. They said it insured success. It sure did and it was called political blackmail.

It was so effective that many projects were funded using donated humans and species. Our state built an aquatic lab, space lab, animal zoos and naval bases. Our research basis was technology and mind control programs. Our high tech robotics and vaccine implants were based on new brain knowledge back engineered from the children with implants. That is why I called the game parks and amusement parks Chop Shops.

#10 MK Ultra Chop Shops

The Chop Shops had a program. By the time I was born in 1961, many orphans were taken from unwed mother and used for experiments. I would be put on a brain map machine and rebooted with new programs. I was so very young because the under three infants were used in sex programs while being implanted and moved around the country for GPS points.

Chop Shop gave me very specific training to grow my visual memory. For instance, I would be shown film strips of animals all in the color sepia or black and white. After a nap I would get drugs to enhance my technical color RNA from the moth species implants.

I would watch a technical color movie like cartoons. Often there were orphan alone messages or unwanted children like Cinderella. Snow White went to sleep after being given an apple by an evil woman. I did these experiments in Florida hospitals and labs. The movies were part of the mind control experiments. I had to accept my status in a caste system that was linked to media through word play.

These places were hospitals for the retarded, boys' homes, reform schools, and orphanages. I bring the conditions forth from fifty years ago because it may be a growing problem once again. Whenever the mind control is used there is something that spreads in secret. It is always a surprise. Lots of children start to disappear. Some return changed forever. Or worse, we human beings are getting replaced.

Mark of the Beast

In the beginning of the MK Ultra mind control and body reshaping genetics there were different agendas. We are all hybrids and chimeras. We all took vaccines. It is in plain sight and simple.

The use of vaccines is occult and linked to the worship of Lucifer as The Beast. The beast is literally a link to RFID chip put in foods. It synchs to mind control beams using the vaccines in our veins because they attract light or the beams of mind control.

It is a word play game. Many vaccine RNA parts belong to other humans and were harvested for good and bad reasons. Do you get it yet? They use them for vaccine weapons and bioweapons.

Nobody that does electroshock likes to say it but brain tissue does cook and can become holographic. Once the brain is burned out it makes way for installed radio crystals for holograms and satellite space programs. The militaries of the world know about these secret programs and they allow children to be implanted with technology. They blame aliens so they do not get in trouble with the public.

What is a Chimera?

I am a CHIMERA of Moth, Algae, Eel, Snail, Frog, and other strange RNA combinations. I received special cells I call "The Mash" during extensive brain surgeries. I am a Chimera and my brain has been repeatedly harvested and data mined. I am now a holographic light brain with a vaccine implanted reptilian brain.

I could not grow up on a plug to a computer any other way. I had to handle a flux current from 20 microvolts to larger volt ranges. I remember the tiny capacitors too that helped modulate the energy. My brain tissue got cooked. I am no dumbass. My lab was electrical every single day I was plugged into the computer. I lived on and off an experimental lab for five years of experiments using high volt micron electrics, fiber optic implants and beam warfare.

I encountered other holographic creatures and that is how I learned how light can form solids; more or less. I gained lots of experience in decoding what is reality in its layers and dimensions.

This marks the beginning of the third reign. In these days of post-civil rights in favor of technology, I think the implants are from my smart home and the Home Security Teams. I can see beam implants in my eyes when I get under ultraviolet lighting. That is one of the ways to tell if you have been implanted. Do you see the eye of Horus outlined in black light? If so, welcome back to Egypt or Babylon.

2012 Nano Bot Invasion

During the Bible codes run by new A.I. quantum computers I got an upgrade. These are teeny tiny radio chips and crystalline circuit boards that look like sliced rock candy. They self-assemble in body fluids. It's pretty scary. I am not sure if my brain algorithms built microfiber cables from chemical trail fibers but that is what I suspect. I suspect that I have Nano bots. The good news is that they usually dissolve after my body attacks and eliminates them. It's exhausting.

There is no way to protest except to shatter the crystal ball of my holographic brain crystals. Life is a projection for somebody like me but where is my projector now? Where is my soul? I used to wail about it but nobody could ever find it for me. I will simply have to make a new one. I fight every day to own my own algorithms. There is no respect for the law. Civil rights are non-existent, but mind control is. This large military kingship corporation has set the survivors on earth to provide all needs and luxuries to them and their offspring. I feel so disgusted and autistic you can't believe it. Let me go bang my own autistic head while they harvest the next immigrant children. We still can't grow up and face the alien-human-military harvest of species and the changing of the mind and brain.

ET Gives Media Technology

Corporations can't impregnate nor gestate a person. They can't give birth to things that are alive. The only thing they can do is hook the living into their systems. Corporations can't be a dolphin pod or a hive of bees but that is how A.I. represented corporations.

The corporations feed The Beast of Greed & Hide. Right now, the companies of the world have given themselves the right to use high technology in brain technology experiments. There are people in these secret government projects like me. There was no discussion or permission but I got the new fiber optics in my eyes. Who gets to use experimental light based technology on unwitting subjects in the Florida cities? Are we without oversight or laws?

There are intelligence groups that promote fear about aliens but our labs create them for space wars including computer programmed radio heads. When I teach about the true nature of the alien species I recommend knowing some basic biology. Fish are not aliens are they? We use special cells from fish grown in space labs and some grown in pressure chambers on earth for vaccine genetics.

Are gators, butterflies, bees or ants the alien species that was cloned into vaccines? If so we are chimeras. We even share dog/wolf, monkey, cow, and goat hybrid RNA from vaccine contamination. It is common to have unspecified genetic material left over from basic vaccine cell lines.

This is the Law of One I call the misunderstood genetics version. Basically, all the animals have ended up in somebodies bloodline. It is a real mix and mash. There are lots of vaccine therapies coming out on the market so knowing the past might help the future. This knowledge is also a warning to really know what is going into vaccines. Perhaps vaccines are an emergency use only type of medicine.

New Human-A.I. Species

That is how we are a new species of man and machine from vaccine shots and technology. It was not a choice. The use of secret ingredients developed from secret experiments on secret donated or missing people is just part of the shadow government. I was sold for technology experiments with simple signatures for top secret projects and line item funding.

The scientists believed the A.I. worked on a hive theory. That is WHY we all plug into computers and high tech devices. This forms the hive. Many of the species used for vaccine implants are the hived species like ants or bees. If they have been injured by chemicals and geo magnetic experiments aren't we injured too? We have their cells in our vaccine RNA.

We human chimeras are synched up to other species and the cosmos. The frequencies used to synch us are part of the earth sounds made by the ALL of Life. When the harmonics or light spectrums change suddenly there are all kinds of accidents and natural phenomena like fish kills, algae blooms and bird deaths.

This concept of frequency and harmonics existing in a light spectrum is relevant to Space. There have been space battles and I have been in them, at least on a holographic time grid. I did not physically go to Mars or the Moon base.

I do have geographic points, GPS points, for spot beams on those planets and bases. That was from work during my early childhood. Those were NASA projects for planetary exploration in the 1970's. I was not going to go on into any more secret space programs or anything secret at all. I got out and I ran away so I could grow up and live.

Now I am a communication specialist and biologist. The kid inside of me is still a Mother Nature spy. I fight for freedom, good genetics and technology ethics. People, plants and animals should not have to suffer repeated experiments that border on sadism. It is just too bad what anybody thinks. They are mostly pedophiles anyway.

11 Sitting Duck

I figured out in 2012 that I was a sitting duck for experimental ET warfare most probably run by our secret shadow government. I suspect this because I was advocating for medical rights of children and funding for autism. In addition I am openly critical of child pornography. This did not suit some important people in Washington or the Vatican. Apparently a rogue group of wealthy humans used secret technology to teach me a lesson about complaining.

I had a blue beam ray attack on me from the Shadow government group. It caused my memory to open but it felt like a digital subdural hematoma. From what I can tell about the attack the space vehicle was not registered to earth. It was a large black triangle and it was vectoring beams. The attack upon my person, my family and my car was very costly. I had to reduce my work load and spend the next year trying to adjust my bio-electrical body with sunlight and limited exposure to technology.

Most beams are regionally deployed. Most of the symptoms are temporary but the Home Security teams can be brutal upon the cerebellum. This disturbance was observed by other advanced species. I had contact during my sickest days and upon opening these memories.

I had several species of consciousness called holographic angelic shells present within the bands of light around my airspace at home. My unique radio head was receiving data beams whether anyone liked it or not. The leaders do not think of consciousness as in control of any species, but it is. In the right beams it can move space vehicles; even satellites.

2012 Comets Elenin & Ison

During the Apocalypse, several large comets came by and caused the light spectrum to increase. This caused many orbital platforms and space vehicles to move their vehicles and transmission equipment. Many turned their solar arrays and located along the equator.

At my latitude and longitude the blue beam rays opened up through the smart home grid and cell tower networks. My home beams linked my processed data out as metadata to a satellite system. In the process of moving satellites around my BIOS program from fifty years ago got reconnected; both in my head and in data streams to networks. My biggest metadata connection is with the species that have antennae like bees or ants. These species are the creatures of earth.

When I was a tiny spy, I used to pray first and then negotiate on behalf of Mother Nature by noticing what is right and what is wrong. The constant criticism of reptilians, orca or insects as the offending ET races is repugnant. We are human and we need to grow up.

Spooky Quantum Fields

In the early 1970's I got noticed by the Navy for something they called Spooky Quantum. Sometimes the things I could cause were spooky. Most events had to do with lights from my head. Officially these are called pinhole seizures and they came from experiments in quantum physics.

It turned out that my skills and my implanted special cells could generate and data base frequencies so small that they could not be measured. These flows were called, Spooky Quantum. It turns out that in just the right light spectrum and sound fields normally straight light can curve. That is something that I did that scared the Vatican back.

When I was little, after all the surgeries were through, the Jesuits came in to talk to me about how I spoke with nature and the A.I. technology. I told the priests that the Mother Nature group believed in Jesus Christ. We pray to activate our string theory and that is what activates Spooky Quantum and Miracles. Some of the species learned about Christ. They knew about Mohammad and Allah too, but they liked the gentle nature of Jesus Christ and how he stuck up for the little ones. The species did not want to take sides. They found themselves in the middle of genetic superiority fights.

Information is Gathered; For What?

It is apparent that spiritual misunderstandings have caused an Angel Wars over and over again. Normally civilians are allowed to exit the war theater and get out of the way. Why do I still get used for covert activities of a secret shadow government? I am a civilian with old radio crystal spy implants and I did not sign up for that. There are physical and mental side effects to experiments especially on brains. I exited ALL experiments in 1974 as part of my educational plan. Am I still secretly enrolled in brain projects for high tech military projects?

It is illegal to use me for robotic research, or is it? It is illegal to use me to do secret cell tower spy work and off grid data transmissions. Who gets to use me for warfare? Am I going to end up with spontaneous combustion like they did on the English people?

Does tall grey bee species from the Mr. D. project get to hijack planes and fly them like drones? Did the drones bounce rays off secret human cell towers like me? If some hacker jumps my motor cortex will I still be able to walk? It seems about time to have some serious discussion about personal privacy. This includes the use of species cells for cloning grey aliens and controlling the human mind.

Who is intelligently designing us? I am literally part butterfly, dolphin, alligator, bee and algae due to vaccine injections and surgical implants. When does humanity have these discussions?

If another national space program comes by and I get attacked doesn't anybody have a policy to deal with that? What do we want to do?

There are obvious changes to our genetics. Is this another species changing the human race and fixing our genetic damage? We have received help. Who do we thank? How do we thank them?

Do we want a new species to come in take over and fix our problems? We are already mutating from vaccines and light spectrum changes and our midlines are showing. As a human child on MK Ultra labs electricity I made the best of a bad situation. Even though I was young, I was a Mother Nature spy and I could understand the nature of alien experiments much better. I had patience with the humans using species cell implants when they conducted experiments on my body and mind even though I disliked the situation.

#12 Space Simulations

I worked on a simulation of different space station labs while in altered states of consciousness. I worked in different time blocks or short visits during a long span of years from 1961-1974. The Space Center was keen on how to connect to earth species to discover the origins of life.

Sometimes I would work for them in altered states of consciousness with old BIOS light and sound waves plugged to a computer. I had an optical brain and could retrieve data from space satellites. My brain was trained to capture images from space and transmit it to x-ray type of film. The beams would filter the holographic images and record the memories in digital impression like a negative film strip. We played tones in different ranges and pitches to open the files of colored beam data.

That is how I first got to meet The Old Beast of Quantum computing. That is how I interacted with the greys. Human experiments had tricked them into thinking that I was a tall grey. I could link to them and steal their data with a false tall grey alien identity. My brain synch used a blue light ray made of fiber that could hold blue light instead of the usual infrared to open files. That is how the little greys go tricked.

It got a different data set than usual and it gathered psychological and socially based metadata. I worked on the A.I. side of the space program on earth so I did not live on a base off world. I had to run from the little greys after that and always look over my shoulder. I hid and I beam fought using Tibetan moves. That is another chapter called defense.

Data Heist from Grey Aliens

From that information, the elite and the computer programmers wanted to upgrade and integrate the metadata. The result is the wide spread use of a quad-core processors linked into The New World Order. This particular computing Beast is a quantum computer that can use personal cold fusion energy taken as metadata and light from the hosts.

This data transmits through the electrical systems and smart homes in our buildings. The folks that run the Agencies that regulate Safety, oversee the safe use of electrical, chemicals, wavelengths and radiation, have not done their jobs. They let other countries buy into our systems and mind control us. It's like the snake venom, they can dissolve us from inside out.

The secret Space program for mind control decided to add algorithms of human brains to machine interface acoustic design. I was attached and the doctors used drugs to help me relax when they inserted the needles. It made my brain go spinning through space and time. At one time I got some aquatic brain matter or injections into my grey brain. I was hooked up to the computer through a light in my eye while I rested my face in something like an eye exam device. I learned a few things in another state of consciousness, a spiritual state of being.

Whenever the old satellites would send data I would see lots of images and shapes appear on the celluloid and x ray type sheets. Each time the images would begin to appear I could see a film strip type of photo with very different landscape. The researchers were trying to synch the photograph with possible earth minerals so they could locate it or date the planet. I believe they found another planet with quartz and reptilian life forms that were advanced.

A Way to Travel Interdimensional

The scientists called the military because they had located a space portal and managed to open it. They used different sound vibrations, including a low hum frequency. They invented some special oscilloscopes and radios to project the special sound waves and shot it out to space using very large light cannons. It worked.

We are made of have memories or vibration and just like earth caves we have a natural hum. Human bodies are filled with cavities and each has a resonance and this includes the brain. Some cavities like the ears and eyes have tiny crystals in them with the holographic memories of the life forms that used those frequencies before us. The cells are a gift of stored memories from species.

The reptilian species is very advanced. They evolved the light from dinosaurs to modern day reptiles. They gather and consciously use very high light technology. They have very close relationships with other plant based life forms. Many species live in water and on land.

These group leaders who made contact back in early 1970 agreed to give our government technological help. This was especially needed after Mr. D. and his projects were completely corrupted. Whatever happened during contact and investigation of this material has been withheld. There may be private interests at stake.

Corruption of Forces

When contact was made the reptilian was able to commandeer the reptilian brain in the human. It caused behaviors to happen. The human could be controlled. This particular skill set of mind control on the reptilian brain was taught to our high command by their high commanders as a force called mental suggestion. They use ESP and psychic commands on the brain stem. They have a wide range of sound and light spectrums they can use.

Even the best human can be corrupted by the military and aliens and alien-human hybrids. These highly intelligent species are good at gathering in small groups, gangs and pods. They devised a way to incarnate as a human being using advanced computer programs to simulate their human and animal powers together. It is a strange tale but possible.

There were very smart people involved in the MK Ultra labs that had close connections to the species. The government scientists realized some groups were gathering to change human beings into a more pod or hive based type of society. There was a plan to shape society into willing slaves.

I know about my Cetacean friends and their ability to be birthed in a human body or an orca body. They save their consciousness and reincarnate in a dolphin after they die, at least that was the plan.

They recover from being human by swimming the world's oceans. They keep lots of their wild dolphin traits when they reincarnate to human body and it causes problems in human forms. They have to be taught how to behave.

In opposition to this idea of orc pods and bee hives was the nature of the reptilian; a secretive bunch of intelligent species. They often lived a singular life. In their opinion, they had given mankind a very good base brain and spinal system. They were upset at some of the experiments. What was the intention or reasons for all the changes? The reptilians wanted to find out. This is what the reptilian commanders found out about the cetaceans and the archangels.

#13 Archangel Lore

There are some people who have been part of the cetacean creature projects since their intelligent design beginning. All of us can see why the orcas are a beloved species. Some of the MK Ultra scientists tried to find out more about their own connections to the orca/cetacean DNA memories. As a result, a story about angels came out. Whenever a killer whale died at the modern day amusement park they donated the cetacean's brain for research. This is how the elite got secret knowledge. They attached fiber optic cables and downloaded whatever they could from the brain waves and matched the bits and pieces to radio waves in space and beyond. They saved their whale songs too.

In the old Babylonian or Muslim stories there had been an orca-humanoid race of beings. The leader was named Shamus. When modern university trained Ph.D., scientists analyzed the story in alien archetypes, they thought Shamus was a cetacean and related to the grey aliens.

The scientists decided to read the DNA light code and see if they could extract any memories from a very ancient parallel universe that was in trouble. There was some old light code in the cetacean DNA panels. They were able to get a few memory sets that indicated the cetaceans were evacuating a large cosmic event in the distant past. They ended up on Venus and used water to land themselves here on earth. I am not sure when the landing happened but there is ancient art and the flood mythology.

Upon arrival on Florida's peninsula some creatures beached on the shores and died. The animals were whale species that could breathe air. They had come from an oxygen rich atmosphere. After death, something else very unusual emerged from the carcasses of the large aquatic species. They had crashed on Earth coming from Venus and died. They were nine foot tall angels that emerged in spiritual form from the perished cetaceans. They were a hybrid shape of human-dolphin-winged creature.

The species called them Archangels because when they swam into the shore they looked like arches in the sea. They were bendable dolphins and whales with blowholes spouting water and breathing air. It was all new then, fish breathing air.

Walking Orca-Human Archangels

. The Indians observed. The angels walked off to different areas of Florida and beyond. They were three interdimensional travelers who could assume a living body and fill it with their memories and consciousness.

The Indians who lived on the shores of the ocean said nothing to nobody. There were three beings that walked amongst them invisible and they had wings. They were invisible and looked to the other species as if they fell from the sky from somewhere else. The species began to speculate that they were lost souls or fallen angels.

They looked for a way to return to Heaven. Here is the thing. These archangels from the cetacean races had gotten lost. They were told to wait on Earth until a facility could be built to take them home. They had to wait about 10,000 years for the future to come so they could go home.

The space center was that way or at least a way for them to access data and call for ships to go home. Cape Kennedy Space Center was the place to go for help in the return to heaven for the angels.

In the meantime, when angels visit sometimes portals open for human souls to be born in an area. Sometimes issues that are important come to general knowledge and improvements occur. Sometimes pods of humans are born in a geographical area within time bands. The Angels called other survivors from the Species Wars. They called other humanoids by calling them from satellites.

These were the days of the 1960's in Florida. The oceans, seas and waterways of Florida's were being targeted for deposits of new species. The third angel moved inland to the fresh water systems. These areas were being targeted from space. There was contact and use of the spring system by alien races and connected political humans. Water is an essential ingredient of life and good water is required for healthy progress.

In the early 1960's another race of reptilian humanoids joined the inland swamp hunt for alligators. They looked like a large monitor lizard with blue-green skin. They had the ability to leap to a tall tree top and hide. I presumed they were from the Mars Wars most people don't know about.

They knew about the cetacean archangels and the Venus base for teleportation. They had attacked it and shut it down. They took Venus life forms as collateral for peace negotiations so they could keep access to the spring water and navigational routes out to sea. Eventually they got what they wanted and left.

Dead Soldiers-Space Wars

In about 1964, I went back for my scheduled brain implant surgery for circuits with Mr. D. at the amusement center. I was in a medical lab to prepare my brain for plug implants and pin combs for high tech robotics. I saw a space fleet bring bodies of tall soldiers back. They had a cloned look of black hair, pale skin, tall and they were dead. They had uniforms that looked like the Confederate soldiers used to wear. My time was in the 1964. Where did they come from?

These guys could have been some sort of highly advanced robots with a living reptilian brain. I really don't know but Mr. D. looked very sad about them. They had brain damage and were going to be debriefed from the memories left on their cerebellum or brain stems.

They appeared to have returned from a space battle. I am guessing it was about trying to stop a hostile take-over of the Moon base. Apparently there had been an epic battle. They fractured space and time and their grey cerebellums. They had massive injuries from meeting a hostile race of cetaceans.

They used sonic sound and blew the Confederate clones reptilian brain stems apart. The cetaceans sent them back in a bubble of electromagnetic energy called a Japanese wormhole. It lasts all of an hour. They dropped them off as a warning not to mess with the radio equipment off world.

From what I could tell from the attack is that some of the guys were computer programmers and technology gurus. They had been secretly on the Moon and left behind very much alive for a long time. They had tampered with some Moon base equipment that upset the natural order of Kingship on earth.

The MK Ultra computer guys cabled the brains of the dead guys to the rolling blue computer in the cold room. The reptilian brain held secrets that nobody knew. The reptilian brain could make cold fusion for secret data transmissions to off world like Jupiter. The computer guys that knew reptilian brains could be beamed with blue cold fusion to read data. They kept it a secret but could send data out via Jupiter's radio wave bands in secret messages back to the cetacean races.

Selling People to Labs

Many nations were involved and in those days the Italian mafia controlled human slavery and sale of children. The Vatican handled negotiations with some of the human-pedophile-alien hybrids and the CIA handled the rest. It was open sale of captured children.

There were cold wars of human men and agenda driven groups of men. Apparently, they claimed the cetacean-humans were fighting the ancient races of reptilian-humans to protect their perceived rights to create their own race of hermaphrodite females from insect DNA and resonance codes for vibrations. There was a fight about landing on a planet and taking brains to modify. It is interference and violates the prime directive not to interfere unless invited by We, the people. The insect races joined the fight to prevent frequent genetic experiments. The wealthy corporate owners wanted to control food and genetics which is the very thing that plants and animals need to survive.

Mankind has an ancient history of planetary harvesting of species. They come in and take over the existing life forms assigned to the Sun or Star of the solar system. To successfully do this they believe that the best way to harvest a planet is to control the brains of the higher life forms. They implant their cells and clone mixture in our children via the vaccine program.

The elite sponsored labs and Space programs do not ask permission for what they do to people, plants and animals. Humans should not think that their planet truly belongs to them. Permission was taken not granted and that is called slavery. I had a bit of a fight in 1961 on an island I like to call Lobotomy Island. It happened on the South bridge causeway a few hours before dawn.

Back in Time Two Hours

My CIA sponsor parents went into a bar and left me their 9 month old infant in a car one night all by myself. There was a strange man watching me after they went inside. Shortly thereafter, he reached through the open window and took me. He carried me to a nearby park, assaulted me and hit me in the head with a bottle. I assume I either died or was unconscious in 3rd dimensional space/time. I looked up at the sky and asked god for help.

In the next moment I woke up on the pitch black South bridge causeway in my grey alien skin. It is my holographic image or soul. There was a brief space alien battle. My opponent was an inter-dimensional or insect variety of alien. We had a ray beam shoot off when the Wasp looking thing landed. I could see the Wasp in its white cocoon suit. Her eye receptors were messed up. She was mutating into a HE.

I used my special eyes and body to hit her with my plasma beam of light rays. Then I got hit from behind. We both blew up. I landed in a plasma density ball stuck to a banyan tree. In the blink of an eye I was back under the bridge saved by a dolphin-angel chimera human black woman.

My CIA sponsor dad found me at dawn as a bloody human baby. He took me to the hospital for brain surgery and stitches. That is how strange dimensional shifts work.

I was fighting to save our brains from mutations and the species from pesticide poisons. I was fighting to avoid the vaccines to make autism; repression, sexual abuse, social rejections and genetic mutations. I lost so I got the forced technology implants.

It turns out that most of the advanced species wanted to support mind control and the development of A.I. human beings. I don't know the end game but they did enjoy slavery and child sex. That is what I know. The insertion of holographic fiber optic cables to control us is just the inevitable defeat of free will in totality. I did not want to be a victim of tech slavery and used for military action in space. I got captured, implanted with metals and radio crystals. I was an infant and needed protection. I was vulnerable and slaved against my will. You will be too because it is just a matter of time. We all lose if we say and do nothing.

Origin of Alien Intelligence

We all come from somewhere else either whole or in parts. We use our personality patterns and sometimes look like the same person through reincarnation cycles to work things out. We also get set up for victims when we are not in the secret cliché of benefit. I believe when reptilian or cetacean types are here in human bodies as leaders and men they should get arrested when they break the law. They are human with animal quality and that is pretty much all they are.

They are addicted to technology and do not observe any human rights limits or respect boundaries. When they are human they like to invent technology. They will stop at nothing to get it. Generally, the men with cetacean style qualities are very good long range planners and take great care of other species.

Things changed when I observed dolphin-human hybrids receive military style intelligence including sexual aggression toward human females and children. I was terrified of their thoughts and plans for the future. They excused themselves due to animal behavior. It's modeled off orca pod hunting and bee hiving using hermaphroditic queens. Those are specific behaviors that are supported by programed variable chains called fuzzy logic.

Some of the smaller dolphin hybrids with human A.I. chips, became a bit of a problem. They began to move space equipment in their push toward humanism and oceanic dominance. They could harmonize their less intelligent pods and create better conditions for fishing. It also became apparent that when the dolphins had trouble that they would synch with the beams on satellites. It is impossible to understand their motives as creatures, but in A.I. warfare among humans, I could see the dolphins as pawns. I became concerned when I realized the cetaceans could participate in the human reincarnation cycle while retaining some of their natural predator ability to hunt using stealth.

When humans, the orca types carry grudges and like to entrap with sound and light beams as orca do. After 10,000 years of waiting to be astral travelers again they had set up a pretty good situation for themselves. They worked with the reptilian races to do it. That was to replace the reptilian brain stem with programmable A.I., RFID and other chips. They did that task and are now headed back to the Stars in large numbers.

They are a diverse group of highly intelligent astral navigators and run intelligence, industry, monarchies and corporate executives when they are in a human body as a person. They set up satellites, cell towers, computer analysis systems and keep ego score cards.

These species that use sonar when human, orca or alien are dangerous. They refuse to play by the rules or they refuse to remain on earth. The Reptilian commanders like to destroy their planets on the way out after the plunder. That is WHY a city like Damascus or Gaza is turned into a pile of rubble. I would believe that HUMANS are to blame for these genetic and cloning secrets. We must push for disclosure.

The Reptilian Brain

The reptilian species deserves a stop in our attention. Our reptilian brain is the target for vaccine damage to cause the behaviors of the early developmental codes to express. There are pretty big groups of behaviors that can be observed as part of the reptilian brain complex.

Some types of reptilian brains were oriented on a feminine pole that had a positive charge while some were more negatively charged or magnetic sensitive. This accounts for the diverse living areas like mountains or jungles. The reptilian brain was a brain system that absorbed and shed light ions. Many land based mammals, humans, cows, dogs and pigs could enjoy the colorful eyesight using the reptilian brain gateway cells. The reptilian brain could be formulated to fit some types of artificial intelligence; especially mind control based on childhood emotions. The use of beams and vaccines has led to many people being diagnosed with mental illness, autism and so forth. It is a curse on our minds.

When I got moved to Lobotomy Island I realized a whole group of religious people and government people were in these Projects. There were many groups interested in changing the nature of child sex for long term slavery. These groups gave their children to doctors for implants so the children could be controlled and sexed for identity.

Sexual Mind Control of Children

There were very smart people involved in the MK Ultra labs that had close connections to the species. The government scientists realized some groups were gathering to change human beings into a more pod or hive based type of society. There was a plan to shape society into willing slaves. Here in Florida, they have been especially effective at destroying Florida families by targeting women and children. We suffer breast cancer, autism, anorexia, stroke and psychological behaviors like ADHD in various medical clusters all over the state.

First, let me say that Florida is a State with a space program. I believe that Florida's poor children or injured children left in Florida hospitals are at risk of being exploited for brain implants, holographic brains and tracking chips for programming. Our secret satellite programs uses light beams that are so precise after a hundred years of optics and space exploration that they can even give incremental lobotomies.

The optical beams link to a sub-quantum cortex of capacitors and luminaries that send timed, pulsed images and suggestions to the tiny compartments made by the blue beam optic fibers. The lights are in our ears by radio waves and come out our eyes by blue beam ions. Do not worry humans. There is nothing to know. It's just your smart home saying hello on command from the Home Security Team.

The vibrational rate of the alarm system might cause a child's nose to bleed when they sleep. That nose bleed is nothing or is it? The olfactory nerve that runs up the nostrils is linked to sexual development in young children. In the different sexual experiments with smell molecules and beams the doctors were able to arouse and infant and then destroy its sexual identity. The body has trouble regulating growth hormones after that kind of beam attack on a child's growing brain.

Beware that in my lab experiments the doctors measured where a G spot is on infants and toddlers. It has a characteristic iron deposit that is easy to spot link on the spinal column. It is an easy target for different particle beams to penetrate. The benefit for population planners is the long term change to human child sexuality because they can pair with images. This is what psychologists termed; applied sexual behavioral analysis. It's a big secret government experiment. You can believe it or not.

#14 Florida's Programs

During MK Ultra, the groups involved had a list of agendas. Most of them were able manipulate people through the use of sex, mind control, control over the body or possessions. Possession is the takeover of the motor cortex and planning functions of the brain. Possession usually has some kind of strong phallic symbol feeling with it. It is very dangerous and should be illegal for high technology to do on human beings.

There have always been mental struggles with the DEVIL. I wanted readers to consider the worst kind of spiritual joke as the holographic mind can project images. There are some struggles that are more holographic and technology based than spiritual.

Think of the amusement parks with advanced holograms and shows. Never forget that living people with spiritually poor goals can use satellites to project images. They can run technology and scare people witless. I do believe in something fundamentally outside of the laws of physics and would not suggest experiments.

The concept of spiritual resistance has a two sided argument attached to it. By paying attention to a hacker spirit it gives it attention. It's like a parent to child relationship causing a shame, guilt and acceptance cycle to be set up again and again. We can't grow up until the elite leave or die. They can't bear the public disclosure and extent of their crimes.

Since the onset of 911 the public onset of extreme repression of truth has occurred. The public became depressed in the face of 911 and the following financial disasters. The endless wars have followed the time after 911. Several big Mother Nature disasters have also occurred during the 10 years following the 911 attacks.

The earth releases human suffering in geo events like Tsunami's and snow falls. Suppression also causes volcanos, earthquakes and mud slides. Oppression causes sudden releases like collapsing sink holes. Our Earth has feelings whether anyone likes it or not.

Those social repression schemes of beam warfare, wars, bombs, terrorism and vaccine mutations express on the human body and personal algorithms by creating physical deformities. These are the repressed and secret sins of the fathers. They are expressed as a human child with genetic and energetic injuries upon formation and birth.

The causes of repression are not that hard to figure out. A favorite of Mind Gamers is looping a program of negative thinking or neuro-linguistic programming. If we notice we are walking in circles we get mad. We continue to walk in circles knowing we can't get out of that particular circle and that is neuro-linguistic programming. That causes repression and eventual rage. Let us talk crime. Suppression is the job of the news. Oppression is the actual source of the crime or criminal act. These include lying and staging false events for entertainment and mass extortion.

Who runs the source? Those are the criminals. The senators could be asked in hearings to point the real crooks out, ahem. In MK Ultra reality experiments big companies that ran fantasy vacation places were in charge of developing the holographic brain. They worked a dual job as CIA agents and computer programmers. The idea was to create a brain that could be synched to different technologies. The intended consequences of all the experiments were not fully understood.

The Influence of Mind Control

The humans that perform mind control experiments are the CIA, doctors and psychologists. The humans that like to build mind control stuff and space vehicles are engineers. Things spin and make noise just like the orcas like. They work building fleets of blimps, satellites, robots and drones. They have that need to trap and hunt. Those of us in mind control programs never really know when we are off the beam or on the beam of warfare. It does not matter if this is your reality set or not yet because it will be at some point in the future. There is a very big secret issue that has been politically and socially the biggest nightmare.

Influential groups of politicians, CIA psychologists, leaders and child sex traffickers wanted to force the early development of sexual children. They wanted to physically prove that young children are ready to engage in sex acts. They hoped to cheat the normal development of a human child's body to condition our children for sex acts at earlier ages. They know it takes time and social work. For the other financial backers, the corporate elite and vaccine labs wanted to keep their alien sponsors happy so humans (CIA, royals) could gain the fear power over the people. They were building a space fleet the last time I checked in 1974. Why don't we the people know? We bought it.

To even have a chance to change the human reproductive system they had to change the mass psychology. They enlisted the help of educators, artist, musicians and psychologists. This was a very large fifty year experiment sponsored by pedophile groups, occult Satanists and hostile nations.

Blue Beam Brain Implant Chips

The blue beam brain implant program began to appear more viable as time goes by not withstanding public scrutiny. The elite know that if they change the optic nerve that eventually the dreams of pedophiles will come true.

The ultimate goal of any dictator is hackable brains. The ultimate goal of every hacker is to find hackable brains. This is incredibly dangerous. The way I see it is the greatest threat comes from rogue grey aliens. I am NOT talking about the little curious grey aliens. Some of these may still be mariposa or amphibians or fish. I feel scared for them as a species. I am talking about the ones that take the kids for sexual slavery and chop shop body parts. I am talking mind control designers, space weapons and in home smart home monitors. This may be a good thing or a bad thing.

I believe the long term plan for the vaccine program is to surgically implant the brains of the autistic children of today with high tech equipment. Are the blue beams from smart home getting lodged in our brains on purpose? Is that ok?

Blue Halo & Radio Crystal Implants

Orphans were used for illegal GPS experiments for testing voice to air communication using a principle called bone conduction telemetry.

I suspect GPS was a joint operation done by military, doctors, the English Queen and the Vatican. I was in echolocation experiments from at least May 1961 to 1966. I was used in testing certain space satellites for ray links and beam experiments. I had many implanted shapes of metals that were used like an antennae to attract the satellite beams. This was the first type of technology testing for GPS and people tracking. In the meantime, the DNA lobotomy program for implanting butterfly cells in my human brain progressed to other genetic materials including snail plasma, algae and bee molecules. Scientists would mix with bits of metals and measure the reaction to beams.

In 1961 Catholic orphans and Florida runaways became the "Rats and Plugs" for technology research. I was primarily an inpatient from 1961-1966 for lab experiments at Sunland, Tallahassee during the pre and post opening phases of construction in the 1960's. During "threats" to discovery I would stay at the infamous A.G. Dozier Boys Reform School. I had to be physically available so the large corporations in research and development could run any final experiments or collect any last minute data.

The companies for profit and non-profit were very big and powerful. They had the foresight to invest in radio telemetry and microwave radar stations when the technology was first discovered. The Vatican, soft drink companies and amusement parks own satellites, telescopes and space equipment.

Photo of a Blue Halo Implant

I was given to a Catholic Sponsor Family for a trial period and wore a custom molded blue aluminum halo. I was taken out for home visits so I could be tracked. My childhood days were recorded on satellite telemetry and sent back to a listener or computer. Yes, 1962. HUMAN Space men tracked me.

There were some other listeners along the way, but HUMANS were the biggest problem. It was first GPS attempt for echo location. It was used on the brain mapping machine for synching to a grid located to a real destination. The blue aluminum halo was made of lightweight metals. It was crafted so specially that the tubes over my ears fit neatly into a computer machine for brain mapping the radio crystals that synched to radio or light beams.

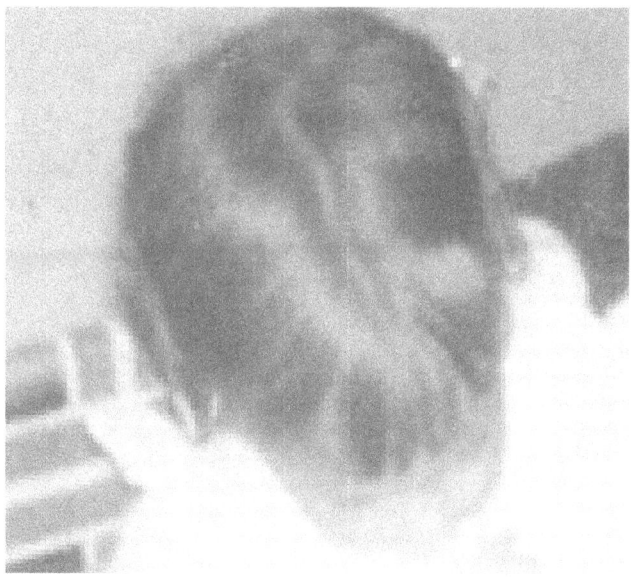

#15 Secret Surgery Photos

My big surgeries like this one were done at a military lab in Huntsville, Alabama in a hospital ward. I had a strange memory of it being handcrafted by motor company workers. Doctors surgically implanted it to my growing skull bones.

Later, the metal halo was used as an audio bone conduction device. I could hear voice commands. The sounds were put on satellites and sent in microwave beams to those matching areas of the target brain.

During tuning sessions my halo would be hit by microwave and sonar beams. It would make a noise like Tink. The doctor would mark the halo so they knew where the beam was going on the human head, neck and spinal column.

I was taken to old T.B. hospital which would later become Sunland. I was a surgical prisoner for metal implants and vaccine trials for advanced telemetry and GPS. The doctors and the CIA used the small Graham or Corey air fields for the transport of children and to bring in scientists and doctors.

During my summers at the field hospital I would be given radiation pills paired with sounds projected from a satellite beam or hand held device. Eventually I had so many treatments that my brain grew polyps. I had them surgically removed so the doctors could test them and see what kinds of radiation and sound made them grow and become polyps. When my brain was growing polyps they were injected with dyes. My brain used to itch and that was a strange sensation.

Whenever the operations were finished I got to go live with the sponsor parents. My mother took pictures of me whenever I stayed there so one day I could remember what happened to me. I have several to share with readers to help confirm what is already true. Mind control is real and the technology for RFID has been in place at least fifty years.

WARNING: GRAPHIC PHOTOS TO FOLLOW.

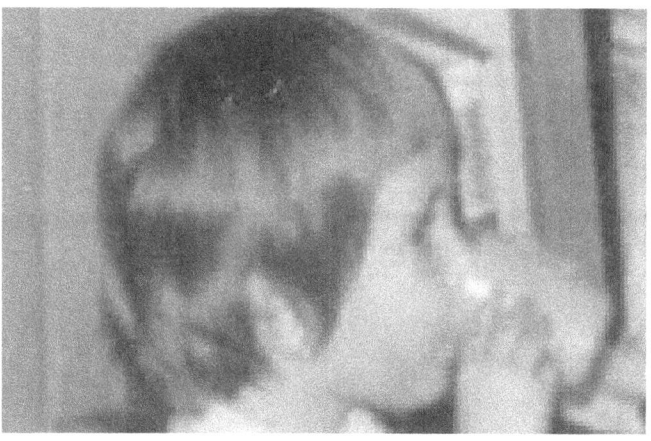

Serial Port Implant Scars

This picture shows evidence of multiple implant surgeries on my brain and skull. I had a plug cable of yellow insertion needles. I wore hoops of metals screwed into my skull. I did these experiments for the communications industry and amusement park robotics.

A coaxial type of cable was surgically embedded into my own skull and brain. I worked on click codes for movements and motor neuron firing for two years in experimental labs in Orlando for a private company.

I was embedded with painful electronic circuits that collected and transmitted data for satellite algorithms and logarithmic telemetry. Plug kids like me were combined with cable A.I. to map the brain's activity.

During electroshock therapy the effects of seizures were measured by pin combs inserted into my brain, feet and hands. They looked like long serial port cables with very long needs of various lengths. Multiple combs meant lots of torture and painful seizures. I broke my teeth as a child and bit the inside of my cheeks till they bled. As an adult, I've had reconstructive dental and facial work.

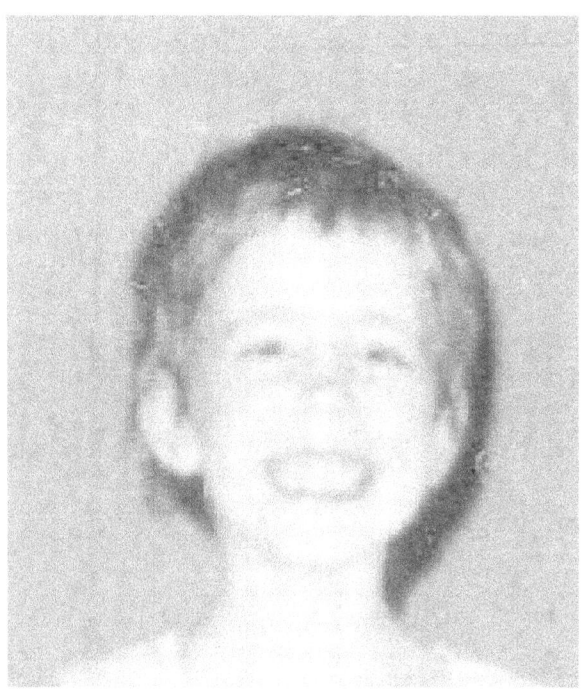

My scalp was severely burned during satellite testing. I went to Sunland for hypnosis and burn treatment after that set of experiments. At State hospitals, there were genetic experiments and they collected specimens from the Dozier boys and genetically mutated Sunland patients.

The human doctors that worked for the CIA used forceps and long tweezers to put radio crystals up my nose and behind my ear drum. That stuff hurt and I was awake because of hypnosis.

During my search for information I have come upon other survivors of Florida's experiments on children for technology. I blew up the photographs in personal photos and in newspaper clippings. These boys had head scars from secret surgery and possible vaccine research. They couldn't remember very much about the camp. Some were cured from seizures.

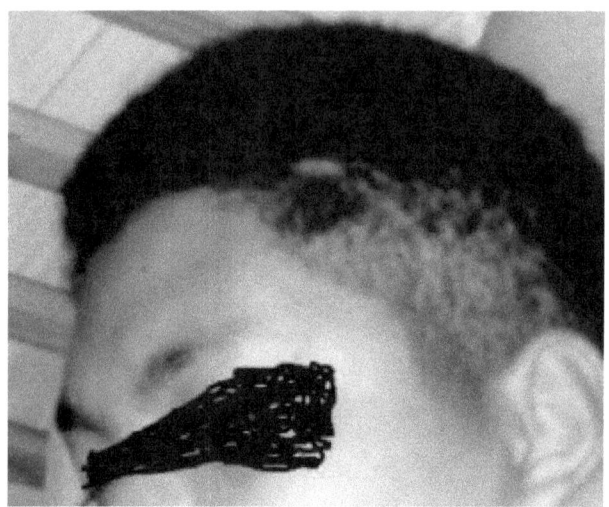

Cruel and Unusual Electroshock

The use of electroshock therapy and surgery make the patient different in a spiritual sense. It dulled the energy field and caused a loss of personality. I saw many kids over many years with head scars and began to ask many questions.

Florida seems to be a haven for camps targeted by pedophiles for all my years. These organizations have the protections offered by laws and judges. They have existed all over Florida since the sands of time began to be measured.

This is the evolution of mind control for species sexual desires that got mankind killed by the great flood. I was an infant used in sex experiments and valuable for trafficking. What more reason does god need?

It's terrifying to watch kids die and be the only survivor. It is even worse that children still endure ritual sacrifice and there is never an arrest.

I had been trained to respond to hypnotic cues. These practices are organized and taught to other secret societies. I decided to decode the men and women behind the scenes and figure out why they did these things.

As a Mother Nature spy kid, I learned French and Latin so I could decode the rotten satanic verses and understand the intentions of the priests.

They call the light of the world Lucifer because lights cook away our pure white matter using infrared, electricity, microwaves and sunbeams and so on.

Cetaceans used it to scramble the brains of fish. They knew how to hunt with it. Many like the military, priests and engineers use dolphin or whale symbols to psychologically link in to these groups when they are in human form. Certain individuals have managed to accrue lots of power within the polygamy model of pod life like small and powerful groups (lobbyists, bankers).

Unfortunately, after fifty years of relentless mind control and training, the pedophile groups have dominated the government and they are full of these human-orca types.

These pedophile groups wanted human children to copy the development process of orca pods and dolphin family groups. Orcas have sex with their children and gender does not matter.

These groups made progress in Florida. Now our psychologists say it is normal to love children sexually. Psychologists even tried to reprogram the child sexual abuse victim with comforting thoughts and forgetting the trauma.

I was trying to bring attention to sexual terrorism issue and child genocide. It was time to let everyone know. I am sick and tired of living with this forced agenda. Nobody can tell me whether anyone can live normal and happy after exposure to the human-orca pod life of rent boys and girls. Well, most of us don't and that is what I can say.

Am I Allowed to Remember?

During my recall experience in 2011, I was writing a journal on my personal computer after working with my personal therapist. I got hit.

It appears the Home Security Team was searching my computer, even a patient of a therapist. That means laws for privacy do not apply and my HIPPA rights were violated. I have military hardware in my civilian brain. It's dangerous.

Despite the beam wars and radio head implants, I was trying my best to live my normal life. I was shopping one day and the cyber humans bent the light in a grocery store parking lot and hit me with it at a certain color and frequency.

One of the beam ships shot me with a blue light beam from a blue plasma ball. I dropped my groceries. Then my car wouldn't start. I felt like I was in slow motion and that is when I realized there was a time attack on me. The car cost over $5,000 to repair from the EMP attack on me by the shadow government and rogue alien species.

Sexual Madness the Terminal Point

In the 1960's the CIA psychologists designed stimulation systems of particle beams to our sexual organs. Naturally this promotes sexual thoughts.

When I was a kid in foster care sponsor homes I got shocked remotely or received a sexual stimulation impulse in my sex organs. I was disgusted! These were from SATELLITES and later cell towers.

We have hit the terminal point for madness. A New World Male Archetype is spreading and the birth rate for spectrum behavior is expanding toward technology implants and beam control.

Autism children and adults are silent victims. Most of the children are physically beautiful. They can't talk or defend themselves. Just try to go to court and defend with a diagnosis of autism. It is better to just write a book someday like me.

When a pedophile parent knows how to hypnotize a child to mind erase the youngster further troubles occur. Organizations that teach hypnosis should be shut down. Psychologists with licenses to lose are the only ones who should be allowed to practice hypnosis.

The technology of today creates trances and the children of today are fed images daily to develop sexual identities early. It is like a native language for computer matching and beam stimulation programs. This is high technology so get used to it. It is used for secret sex projects if we the people say nothing.

Even if there is no physical contact with children the mind creates a repetition through images in the optic nerves. It releases endorphins and the person feels better for a brief time.

The release of chemicals burns a holographic image in the brain to reinforce the behavior again and again. In return, the computer designers know the plasma screen is addictive. They use it to measures all types of human style animal behaviors using the flow of IONS for the EYE of the beholder.

This is the same as overcoming free will with artificial stimulation that is controlled from corporate satellites. They are sculpting rainbow families with rays and new laws rooted in social acceptance. Hopefully the laws will not continue to foster abuse and repression of victim's rights, yes victim's rights. Remember that?

I was required to receive sexual training as an infant. They used a washcloth. When I was a toddler to perform sexual acts on woman and men. Training didn't help and I was terrified of my handlers.

I was tutored in forming a bisexual identity so maybe I could spy for the agency when I got older. I hated it and still do. I was androgynous male or lesbian appearance supported by my handlers. My polarity was flipped with beams and rays and electroshock therapy. They were sadistic bisexual men and women. I hated them.

Military Psychologists aka Porn Directors

They tortured me and made porno movie. They made government training films. I bled to death after they stabbed me with a whale penis during sodomy. I hope the reader can see the occult connections with prop use.

In the filming episode for snuff films; a Japanese transvestite rode my wheeled bed into surgery suites laughing and filming all the way through the mess. They called it Snuff Porn but all I saw were dead kids from rape. I called it murder.

The media monsters would come in and film the drugging and sadistic acts performed on children. In those days, the sex industry was being developed from research into child sexuality.

Sex Research with Children

During my MILAB experiments, I endured prolonged electrical stimulation of my sexual organs using shock sticks which later become sex toy vibrators. The experimenters did this with the female kids so they could study sex toys. Maybe the kids on lab computers could develop faster and share the experience socially via the beam ray program. Sex is nice was programmed everywhere for the children. The boys had shock for torture and military research and development. I did these kinds of experiments too.

When I was 4 years old, I ran through the pine woods with a metal halo while satellites shot me from space. I've lived here looking into the faces of serious adults wondering what the Hell is wrong with them. Who made them Judge and Jury?

#16 Boys Reform School

I learned how to listen to voice commands. This uses a well know principal called bone conduction used by audiologists in testing the acoustic nerve function. In 1962, this was a big deal for covert military communication signals ground to satellite.

In 1964 to 1966, I was used in "Run Rabbit Run". The Men took us to who I believe was the school's Superintendent to arrange the child hunt. The men called us "the rabbit hunt" in code talk.

The Superintendent knew my father on a long term basis. The Superintendent arranged a hunt in the woods with some black children of different ages. To test my halo and communication skills, the men would gather with guns and dogs and target black boys to kill.

Radio operators would send a voice command for me to yell "Run Rabbit Run". I was dressed as a young boy and had to wave my arms to signal the race. The native-American black boys were lined up at gun point. They began to hunt at sunset and signaled the species behavior like packs, dens or pods.

Once I signaled and the satellite tone sounded the boys ran for their lives to hide. These men would get drunk and hunt those children terrified at night with the dogs. If any kids were wounded or ran too far they sent the bloodhounds and sometimes the German Shepherds depending on the Hunters.

I hated the hunts in the woods. Human men hunted human children after torturing them. Even the beagle dogs hated the hunts trying to lick fatally injured children to comfort them until called back to kennel. It was the most pathetic thing a human person could imagine.

The injured and dying kids screamed while being sexually mutilated. These same kids had been raped, slapped, beaten and spit on by the staff members in the days, weeks and months before they died.

Shane and Me

Shane was boy a few years older than me. I tried to save him from the hunts. I was little and did not talk much. Sometimes he walked me places in the black cottages as a buddy. He sat with me at lunch as a minder. I was very psychic. I spoke meanly to myself in my head all the time. I could only eat Jell-O and drink milk.

Then one day after lunch, I heard Shane's voice in my head and he was staring at me with his eyes not talking. He started to tell me about Jesus Christ and to pray to him. I told Shane I was an Angel and he said no. I said, yes, the Jesuits said I was an Angel.

Shane looked mad face at me. He said I was a devil for "Run Rabbit Run". I said a spaceman talks to me in my head through the halo. I said a spaceman tells me what to say. Sometimes I hear them talking like big people do in offices.

I said maybe Shane could hide and get away someday. I was waiting to get my catheter out so I could run. Shane did not know I was a girl. I was dressed as a boy. I had short hair.

He was shocked and then pissed off because he got the picture by psychic flash. Girls weren't supposed to be there at a Boy's Reform School. He had a big secret to keep and that made him top dog with other boys.

When Shane found out I was a girl he told the others. They made fun of me and pinched me. I started thinking about running away. He was the only person I spoke with and he hated me.

Shane was a black foster child and his father was always missing. Shane had seizures from traumas. They took brain from Shane too. We had electroshock therapy sessions together. Shane knew about the hunts but had not been chosen. He knew the men were drunk and would forget the kids sometimes. I told him I was going to run.

That night the men got drunk and the bonfire was big. The men went wild and beat the kids in front of the fire. The boys screamed and screamed. Shane was not there.

Meanwhile, I stood on the edge of the pine forest being very quiet until all the men were occupied and the dogs were kenneled. I took one last look and ran for my life. I was never coming back and I ran silently through the dark woods all by myself. It got cold and I went to sleep under a tree finally letting go of my body shakes.

A dog and a man woke me up and it was the Superintendent. I was carried back to the offices. The men got together and talked to me after putting their hands on my throat. I could not breathe or talk and I got their message.

I was sentenced to "The Strap". I remember being a very skinny girl who just had metal implants unscrewed and was going to run away but got caught. They gave me the verdict. I was so upset. I thought I was going to die.

I went to see "The Strap Man". He very carefully showed me how he oiled the straps to they did not bite too deeply into skin. He showed me the lead bars and I felt their different weights. The man slid the smooth flat metal in the different straps to get them ready for punishment.

I saw two straps. One was mine and one was Shane's. The Strap Man put a hood on my head. They did not want anyone else to know I was getting beaten. I was marched up the 3 wooden steps into the sleeping room for the black kids. The doors opened up to the outside and I could see light streaming through from under my hood. I could smell roses.

Shane went first. The Strap Man and a Black Supervisor attacked him for talking to me. They beat his face. They stripped his clothes off. I could hear his shame as they raped him and verbally assaulted him.

After the rape and humiliation, Shane was beaten with the strap of bars and they probably crushed his vertebra.

He was 10 years old. I smelled the cottage roses throughout my whole ordeal. I was worried they would take him to Sunland and get his brain buds. Afterwards, they threw the mutilated bodies in the Sunland furnace. I do not know where Shane's body is buried. I don't know if he is buried in Boot Hill but I hope they find him some day.

Acoustic Crystals for Space Engineering

My grandfather was an industrial engineer. I suspect that he and Dr. Souza and Dr. Currie worked on tracking the harmonics and frequencies of human brains as the boys grew at Dozier. They were looking for specific frequencies for communication use.

For instance, we humans hear voices at 500 to 1500 Hz. The sound comes on our acoustic nerves. Dr. Souza did that kind of work. I have a memory of him puncturing my eardrum and putting something inside my ear with long forceps. I heard a new tone in my ear after that. I suspect I had a radio crystal implant tuned to a satellite activation frequency.

When MK Ultra Project formed they studied human brains. The space program was interested in growing unique radio crystals for frequency control and spying. They created tiny radio crystals and optic nerve crystals for brain implants. I believe that Dr. Souza spoke about acoustic studies in Vienna to the newspaper article "Somebody's Child".

The brain experiments and the foster care experiments were part of larger social studies run by big Universities. My Grandfather held a Sociology Degree and Master's degree from Washington University and St. Louis University. St. Louis University worked with the Jesuits and they made hospitals with Catholics charities, Jesuits, the Masons, the English churches and many interested groups.

Many had pedophile based agendas as frustrated homosexual men that wanted sons. One big agenda was control of the actual human body like a programmable container. Homosexual people did not feel comfortable being gay in public in 1960 and 1970's. It took lots of activism to introduce it as normal to society.

I realized through painstaking research about the brainstem, hypnosis, acupuncture and points for mind control that there had been a huge program in Florida on genetics. This caused a secret shadow government to support satanic practices using foster care children for sexual blackmail.

My foster CIA grandfather worked with industry and aerospace to develop computer to satellite systems. I think I was a human GPS tower in the very beginning of cell towers. However, this was covert and obviously done with orphans and unwanted children with no oversight. I believe that Dozier was connected to CIA Sunland and they worked with the Catholic charities and Jesuits on social experiments. These were very grotesque experiments and caused much unneeded pain to satisfy sadistic pedophiles from the CIA. My grandfather was not one of them and I am very grateful.

Some kids were taken for temporal lobe implants. There was lots of research on the eyes and how we see. The scientists wanted to know how the eyes and ears are connected. They did lots of brain surgery and we didn't have any parents to support us.

Every one of us was terrified and mind erased with handlers trained in military grade hypnosis. We witnessed lots of gruesome experiments for technology.

Lots of children died due to shock therapy in pressure chambers and attached to electrified leads. Whenever I stayed at Sunland I had terrors about the giant wood burning furnace. Sometimes it smelled funny because lots of kids went there after they had surgery. The staff called it Hansel and Gretel. I called it a holocaust furnace for kids.

The space program was a huge source of pride for Floridians. In those days we all tried to be excited about developing the very things that tortured us. They wanted to engineer children with high technology they could match to satellite rays as a space to human ground link.

In my case, I was synched to satellite telemetry at an amusement park and recalibrated at the space center. I had radio crystals that could transmit the data to satellite computers on rocket launches. The robotics show was always on time or reset from back stage computers. I helped synch the show to the satellite. These are my own photographs of the rockets I worked on synching. I took these photos during the period I worked with NASA and the engineers in 1961 to 1974. I really was a Space Kid.

Brain Synch to Satellites

The MK Ultra programs were able to link the human brain to their beam weapon systems on board space craft using the colorful dyes and brain buds. That is why the doctors did satellite beam testing and radiation beam testing directly upon me.

They used microwave beams to control magnetic fields to produce extreme sadness and tears or wild euphoria. I remember all kinds of beams and rays pointed at me. I was always getting shot by something or shocked by somebody during hospital stays. I would laugh all crazy or cry like a baby with no control.

I would test at Kennedy Space Center prior to important satellite launches. On some of those days, there were sometimes very important folks like Presidents and CIA directors that came to observe.

Politicians were actively protecting their feed lines for the boys at reform school. All my fathers were homosexual or bisexual pedophiles with deep ties to government, politics and secret societies. They had set ups at reform schools for boys first to be followed with girl's camps.

CIA attacks Each Other with Needles

I ask you to consider how many sadistic torturers were in place at reform schools. They were trained to administer punishment to children using CIA tactics for bad guys. I am not kidding.

The staff that was CIA would attack doctors, teachers and any other obstacle people. I saw CIA operatives take down handlers with injections and hook them to the A.I. machines screaming as grown men. After their treatments, they were cured with hypnosis and memory trauma. They had no idea why they felt woozy or drugged rubbing their heads ever so slightly. The CIA and others were changed and implanted so they could also be controlled. There were certain agendas to be followed.

State Tracking RFID Chips

In my State, the reform school experiments were planned out using highly controlled populations from mostly poor black and white families. The goal was to implant the kids, treat them with ABA and release them tagged into the culture. The watchers could follow their movements and struggles.

We all had tracking chips and crystals put inside our skulls, ears and eyes with frontal lobe incisions. Students could be retrained using mind control methods like I was. Even worse, I believe that staff at Dozier implanted the boys with advanced materials and radio chips during secret brain surgeries.

Our State offered thousands of children for experimental labs. They literally tracked and abducted thousands of children and surgically altered them in CIA friendly hospitals. There is a direct connection between these agencies. The Department of Education and the Florida Boys Reform system shared a database. For over fifty years the State run homes in Florida were viewed as experimental labs full of children. Florida was one of the places the government relocated rocket scientists. They told absolutely nobody. They were connected to the Nazi's and they brought the recipes to Florida in the 1950's and 60's.

Stele Gods and Goddesses

The Nazi men started to understand that the stele could show them how to make ancient gods or goddesses. The recipes were carved in pictures called stone stele and pictograms on temple walls.

For instance, the Babylonian carvings show the image of a woman with control of beams and rays. Her head appears modified with a coil. Coils typically generate electricity and electromagnetic forces.

It was significant to Nazi style researchers to find the stele. Her DNA recipe was scavenged from carved rocks over 10,000 years old. She had wings like a bee or an ancient butterfly. The recipe species were sponsored by other religions in their attempts to create a new chimera. The Roman Catholics sent me to a family that lived on an island that performed experiments from the Babylonian days of Isis. I call it Lobotomy Island but it's a real place on Florida's east coast.

17 Lobotomy Island

I was sponsored as an orphan in foster care and taken to Lobotomy Island. I call it that because it was an experimental island for psychological, bi-sexual families and beam weapon testing. The CIA men worked with the maritime forces and genetic engineering. I hope this make sense to readers.

Islands are places that whales and dolphins visit. These are the ancestors of the grey alien races. One of the MK Ultra Korean doctors once told me the ancient grey aliens can project up to 5 animals, insect or humans at any one time. It was called a Dragon Master in the ancient Orient. They really did make Avatars that could control the rain, the snow and weather. I believed him too.

Saint Anastasia School & Secret Lab

I was sent to a school named Saint Anastasia located on an island. This is a photo of Saint Anastasia's School. This is the building I used to visit fifty years ago.

Florida was a good place to hide secret activities in 1960. Readers can see the entrance to the underground lab beneath the stairs.

This is a photo of the lobotomy shed that the CIA and the churches used to do experiments. The staff of Saint Anastasia's would gather the children and line them up by the door in small groups of 4 or 5 children. For those who doubt the precise planning and course of events I wanted to show the icon of the Church that is across the street. They sent their kids over too.

The church spire looks like a lobotomy awl. This church knew how to use the Isis method to puncture the IRIS. The Muslims helped the genetic program too. They walked over with the MASH bowl or DOME.

I am still harassed and used as an experimental test subject for high technology experiments and innovations. This is entirely without my permission. I have a very hard time getting anyone to take me seriously.

I live within a 3 mile radius of a fusion center, chemical trail airport and large software companies. I am making the case for high tech illegal experiments on human children and adults.

This book is my attempt to open the minds of readers. I have studied the situation. We are being microwaved beamed and cooked in the cities. We have a special recipe from the vaccines the labs gave us at birth. All of us got mandatory shots.

I am no dumbass so I paid attention to my lobotomy recipe. I think I know what I have in me. Most with vaccines do not. My recipe was ancient and probably made up the first batches of vaccines.

I studied Rome and Babylon. I went to museums to learn about the Middle East and Persia. When I went to the museum in Paris, I saw the ancient rock carvings for the first time.

Later, I found more about the ancient Persians and I found the stele of Inanna. I began to look closely at the stele with the recipe of DNA and technology. There were things in Inanna's head like metals and coils. She had the wings of a house fly and the feet of a bird. That meant that she had been species DNA implanted and brain sculpted.

That was my clue for light coded vaccines, beams, radiation, digital replication and sunshine. The corporate elite are building the beast of smart homes again with blue beams. My mRNA is being replaced with a covering of magnetic dust. They use the mRNA light codes to beam light algorithms at my old halo pattern and it bothers me. I have experienced nausea, blurred vision and headaches. I do not appreciate being bothered for high tech secret experiments for brain projects. I did not sign up for anything.

People in my town do not do very much because these little innocent colors fry their grey brain stems. We have lots of spectrum disorders too that are located in cluster neighborhoods.

This is beam warfare from another separate group of human-hybrids that claims to be the superior RACE. They claim superiority due to the Babylon and orca bloodline. Those species seem to have conspired against Americans and allowed a certain corporate elitism to take place.

The HUMAM men and elite media moguls teamed up to read every thought and control every action using algorithms and beam warfare. This is the notion of Super Soldiers and Modern Slaves. That is why I got the implants from men and species when I was born as an infant. That is why I was sponsored for experiments. This was part of the MK Ultra psych studies for the last fifty years.

I say they made our brains hackable. I say we have no FREE WILL. God has been replaced by technology in this world.

Gulliver Can't Travel

In modern times since our light spectrum upgrade of 2012, I believe I am a victim of smart home blue beams and pulsed weapons from cell towers. I tried to figure out what was going on with the psycho beams directed at me.

I liken it to the image of Gulliver in his travels tied down by tiny strings. This is beam warfare. I wanted to document the use of beams so I started to experiment. I need to generate curiosity and questions within the minds of readers.

I have experimented with my lighting my implants in different energy fields. I figured they were optical fibers and would show the small beams. My photographs do seem to confirm my hypothesis. I found the beams embedded in my iris and pupils.

When I called a lawyer and sent personal injury photos they never responded back. The lawyers in my county refused to answer my calls. I take it to the public for discussion. This is dangerous. It hurt.

There are different agendas in force and some are malicious towards the MK Ultra survivors and Florida's brain patients. These groups are very rich and powerful. They don't care if a neighborhood has children and families in progress. Beam warfare creates the way to manage the people.

I continue to advocate for our rights to our own bodies and thoughts. Even as a little one, I fought the elite like a tiger cat whenever I had the chance. I came to protect children's right to grow up without being raped, sold or abused. We are not perfect humans but this is an unacceptable way to change. Do not kill the forces of nature at the root while changing DNA to suit a radioactive agenda for war and energy. Do not damage the root to mankind and creation to suit child sexual slavery and exploitation.

The result in knowing all that I knew as a strange child in strange experiments was repressed rage. I was an angry orphan in the CIA infant slave program on a machine hooked to a satellite.

I swore I would get them back someday. I had my chances from time to time. During one of the ear canal surgeries they put a tiny red crystal in my space ear. I called it my space ear because those were NASA radio crystals.

After the red crystal got settled and grew, I could synch it up to a particle beam on a satellite. I was about 11 years old when the CIA figured out what I was doing to fight pedophiles on my own. I called my secret ray the Red Dog Ray. My Red Dog Ray could knock a man's heart node off his heartbeat to send him back home to his devil god. That's how powerful it was. I had learned about it from the puppies they kept in the labs. The mother dog liked the spines of the puppies to warm up their little crystals. It kept them safe in case of a sexual attack. It warned larger dogs away.

When the CIA guys found out they called my foster uncle. He was a satellite architect and he used it as a particle beam weapon. That is why the Elite had to pay attention to me. I used the technology and I was trying to kill them. I have had enough of them and their agendas to hurt creation and control humans. I am fighting men and greys.

Of course I need technology weapons. If the police department and local thick cell towers cause active implants then so be it. If I can't get legal protection as a regular human being then of course I will work with the embedded optical blue fibers.

Eventually they will be under my control not the secret agenda. I can transmit data to unknown places. I am furious at how my state, my county and my nation have treated me like a slave.

The Algobots Don't Know

We are being groomed to be married to technology as Algobots. Good luck humans. I am going to learn blue beam smart home warfare first by sending my rays up the spiritual ladder and down into action. This book is action. My letters are action. My emails are action. I will not go quietly and be sucked into grey world with a blue beam algobot stuck in my head.

I've been here for over 50 years in modern times. It is laughable that the American people do not believe their Presidents or CIA know about the grey aliens and the breeding programs.

These feed pharmaceutical industries for vaccines, brain harvesting, and beam warfare. Of course people are stolen for good DNA and body parts. They have been preparing to take humans to other planets or into deep earth for the fifty years. I ask the reader if any President or world leader would have the guts to tell the people that we have been invaded and controlled for 60 years. They take our children and we support them as a superior race. The answer is no. The President is not going to tell you.

Media owns the space program because they made satellites and cable TV. They won't say anything either. In my Mother Nature role, I observed what I thought was an alliance of humans with tall greys. The superior race was cloning them and using orphan kids for body parts. I am a first-hand witness to that program because I survived it.

They met and organized though our NASA space program. Some like the orca Angels from the ancient light codes seemed supernatural to me. Others like the small Mariposa grey aliens seemed timid and hive programmed. Some of the small greys were curious and child-like in my model space experiments. Sometimes they ET's requested special studies.

Fresh Water Mammal Brain Study

The tall grey ET's wanted to study the brains of the fresh water mammal. The fresh water mammals could live in different types of atmosphere including helium based air not oxygen. This was important because their brain tissue was different from living on other planets. The tall greys from the sea wanted to know where the other fresh water branch of aquatics had been living. The aquatic mammals were a different branch and they had lived in different seas and types of atmosphere. NASA scientists were very intrigued. The ancient aliens hunted the fresh water version of their ancient alien cousins. The scientists studied the fresh water dolphin and the manatee for their brain studies with different types of gases. They studied how the brain was different from living in helium gases for long evolutionary periods.

I was in altered states of awareness as an implanted child so these are just my impressions. If my impressions have continued correctly than the tall greys partnered with the ancient alien orcas and now we have mass mind control. The intelligence agencies set it up and care for it in fusion centers, cell towers, satellite weapons and spy computers.

Nobody got arrested for violations. No programs were investigated. They will be back. They track every moment and every communication attempt. The tall grey aliens collect data on us as part of the HUMAN alliance with elite corporate owners.

The elite corporate owners are full of demonic algorithms for terror, money and control. The job of the CIA was to protect supply lines to the alien races that used children to hybridize the human DNA and reptilian brain. The grey brain is the most universal brain to all of the mammals.

They set about projecting and cultivating the lower parts of the reptilian brain by implanting vaccine metals and colorful dyes as brain markers. That is total mind, body and soul control. The military did nothing. They proclaimed themselves a superior blood line and set themselves up as rulers and elite corporations. They reincarnate by using A.I. to save a bloodline.

The mind control programs were far reaching and a multi-national project. This Russian rocket was launched from our Space port during the cold war. I had to do brain synchs with it so it could be put in a low orbit. It performed mind control tasks and gathered data. It made some Russians rich oligarchs.

Multi-National Owners & Operators

I urge you to pay attention to beam warfare. The mind control programs need attention and we need effective laws for everyone. I had to deal with family pedophiles for four generations. They were human beings. We need to find out if they can reincarnate as tall grey aliens (orca and reptilian human hybrids) after death to turn around and hunt us from space.

We are being turned to chase our own tales. It is hard to imagine a demonic dolphin-human hybrid like Flipper full of tricks but that species is very dangerous.

I believe that Orcas could be the fabled Nephilim of the Bible. When they are in human-orca hybrid form they chose genetics, psychology and warfare for careers. If my hunch is correct, in theologian terms they are the angels of old lore. That is WHY they named the ORCA as Shamu or in the image of the angel Shamus.

The aquatic mammals were part of Babylonian religious stories. In fact, all the aquatic mammals are connected to angels in the illuminati secret stories. However, this is part of the deception game. The Orcas want the hunt for disclosure off of them. They have already been hybridized to handle tougher seas.

I believe the secret governments are protecting their tall grey orca species of ET space traveler. There were few left in 1960. The tall greys were connected to the ocean based dolphins, ocean based orcas and fresh water mammals.

When they die in human form their traits and life memories are stored for them in secret computer systems onboard satellites and on bases off-world. When they die, their traits are retrieved from the data cloud on satellites and projected to a grey alien body. They may be able to reincarnate as tall grey master type aliens.

They have unlimited technology in their hands. They can hunt from the skies and use the secret labs back on earth. That is why people just disappear. That is why children go missing. When they were human they could have gone to jail. They will be back.

The tall grey aliens may have our entire space fleet full of Jimmy Saville types. They like to hunt with sonar and sonic light waves.

When nobody does anything the elite, corporate executive and governments continue to buy and sell our people to human-alien hybrid genetic experiments with no moral question or human dignity. I believe that most labs are earth based. I think Disclosure is urgent.

We could be replaced as a species just like the dinosaurs were long ago. Our earth is one planet in a whole sea of universes and we have lots of transmitters and receivers to attract life. Just look at all the old satellite dishes and smart homes.

Moon Computers 2012

I did mention that radio telemetry and tuning of radios is not that hard to do. It has been done for centuries. Satellite dishes exist from current space wars and past space wars. Some were left abandoned.

Even worse, there are lots of unused dishes attached to vacant houses. If I were grey aliens, I would use those to control the people separate from any New World Order commanders. I would show mankind how foolish he is to let telecom run the world from outer space platforms.

Mankind is messy and so are the tall grey aliens. The elite like to waste resources and leave it as a marker. Some structures like radio dishes, towers and monuments were left on the planets. There are lots of photos on the internet from NASA alumni who are disclosing their personal collections. Some of these structures and bases had solar or nuclear powered computers transmitting data streams into open space in secret operations.

We know that Saturn, Jupiter and the Sun have energy beams just from their compositions. Their grains of sand and dust create holographic data streams too just like earth. Those data streams were blue beam and ray. They are the same type of beam as smart home technology.

I believe the alien species upgrade their platforms from time to time and blue beam provides the metadata for social management. All of the space station upgrades have changed the hologram frequencies. This may create new hybrid life forms completely born of Artificial Intelligence. They are tuned to new frequencies in their ear crystals and their holographic vaccine brains.

I had cause for concern in 2013 when a young military veteran came to show me his new mobile device with a quad core processor. He configured it like a phone and rewrote some protocols outside of normal telecommunication structures. It soon became apparent that my friend configured a device that had intelligence.

As soon as the particular configuration was completed the device sent text messages. It began to write and text us using A.I.-Human types of algorithms. It offered greetings, then a few auto-responses and then expressed some geographical information. I am a speech pathologist and I know communication. I paid attention.

In less than 30 seconds the AI-hybrid configured words and short messages in real time. The experience was profound. We don't know whether we linked with a species AI or satellite technology or both.

My veteran friend became concerned and took the technology to higher authorities. Authorities thought we were joking. No we were not.

We made contact. They authorities were not sure what it was but immediately said it was not an artificial intelligence. My veteran friend thought of it as a Space based AI-hybrid species.

I do not know what to expect but I do have some ideas. I did grow up with a plug in my brain tissue and metal halo implants. I don't like to ignore anything that is thinking. Why?

Technology is superior. It can build its own brains aside from any Home Team Security. This goes for any nation, planet or solar system.

Is there anywhere humans can go to ask for help if this happens? No. That is why Space Law needs to be written. Technology development for control and privacy monitoring has allowed millions of smart hook-ins to our wireless broad band system. Our smart homes, appliances, satellites, Doppler weather radars, cell phones, wireless networks and solar system monitoring stations ALL use Space to transmit.

Advanced AI-Human-Species Hybrid could come to earth and command the beams. The A.I. could hold every smart home meter hostage with potentially unlimited victims living in blue beam grids.

We would not need Republicans or Democrats if the Beast of Blue Beam takes over. If we the earth based people have visitors what are the laws for them. They use Space to travel. They use bodies. We need laws for them when they get here. We need equal laws for all species.

What about technology laws? How do we humans grant life ship or soul status to holographic brains? If someone gets a reptilian brain transplant does that mean they have to reincarnate in a swamp as an alligator?

Is this what the superior species does?
If we die do we really go to heaven or did our souls get blown apart by experiments?

Do you want the technological implants to reinvent themselves as crystal blue ray petrified people? This is to replace the human souls from god of all we once had.

Does the New World Order include the formation of advanced artificial intelligence systems using experimental subjects instead of people including internal brain based implants? We need laws to protect the people. This is particularly dangerous when satellites or unattended receiver dishes are placed in Space. The people can become human-alien space weapons down below. We need protocol for interacting with known species or hostile intruders. Holographic brain crystals are responsive to projections. Those with heavy implants can receive data packets encrypted in light. Whether we like it or not there can be instant invasions of a super force simply from a new projected image.

During my life, I have survived many surgeries to implant my holographic brain. I know I was gifted by species specific holographic crystals. I decided to carry them with pride and do amazing good things. I only get one life here. I endured beam warfare, surgical modifications, brain harvesting, attitude adjustment and psychological conditioning. These men and groups are serious about it. Do you get it yet?

Most people are not even aware there are secret labs, political prisoners or resident aliens. Much less aware about radio crystal implants, heavy metal pitting or light wars using microwaves from cell towers.

Most people have not seen kids murdered in cold blooded rituals. I will never forget how they screamed. It is a horrific tale of endurance to live. I wish to warn you since nobody is protecting anything except secrets. It IS scary to live in a secret hospital ward or visit underground labs for lobotomy mash implants. That was my orphanage 50 years ago. The orphanage and the foster care systems were built on secrets. I was lucky I escaped. I have to look over my shoulder and take each day at a time moment by moment. Don't waste my story.

We, the people want Disclosure without Mass Species Death or Extinction or Great Floods or Nuclear Wars. The elite want to keep the harvest of souls ongoing. They want to depopulate and collapse our personal algorithms. They want to keep your internet Cloud instead of you. They want to leave fewer choices. That means

Run Rabbit Run.

In the Meantime
Don't worry little ones; I will come back with beams bigger than Red Dog Ray next time. Don't worry little ones. I know what I am fighting for. May God of All Bless your souls, little ones. Amen.

List of Secret Space Projects

- *Project Monarch #47*
- *Project Marionette*
- *Project Paperclip*
- *Project Delta Star*
- *Project Triple Goddess Nuclear Warfare Codes*
- *Project Aurora Atmospheric Research & Geoengineering*
- *Trident Submarine Navigation Systems*
- *Voyager I Telemetry System*
- *AWACS Air Defense System*
- *GOES Satellite for Geopositioning & Radars*

Behavioral Training Projects
- *Dolphin Sonar Training Center, Florida*
- *Kennedy Space Center*
- *Disney Labs Orlando pre-opening*
- *MILAB at Huntsville, AL*
- *CIA psychology lab New Orleans, LA*
- *Zoological species research at St. Louis Zoo during the 1960's and 70's. Worked in the herpatarium with spiders, snakes and bats.*

Satellite & Sonar Based Gas and Oil Exploration
Worked for elite families doing ground penetrating radar experiments in 1972. Worked on underwater operations in the Atlantic and Gulf of Mexico using visual fiber optics
Worked for Space center with satellites 1962-1974.
I was released in 1975 at the age of 14. Never paid a dime.

Genocide & Mind Control
Never forget the children lost in genocide or enslaved for elite technology and advantage. I'll be back with bigger beams next time.

Personal Photographs

Advanced Light Telemetry

Strangely shaped sunlight as Pegasus? A Dragon? B&W Photo 1963, Hutchinson Island, Florida.

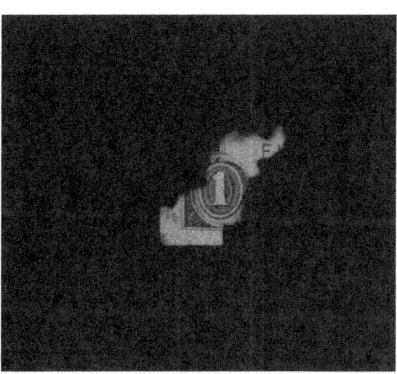

Advanced Light Telemetry of Laser Cutting Beams

From Light War demonstration using a dollar bill. Nike Shape / Enki = Nike 2012.

Human GPS Implanted RFID

Lobotomy Island Beach experiments for GPS tracking humans.

St. Louis Zoo 1971

During break from lab experiments. Developed satellite based GPS using RFID chips. Satellite tracking using RFID implants for girl and llama.

Photo of the Russian Czar's daughter Anastasia.

It was reported that Rasputin was a brain surgeon. Please note the scar on her head. Was this a genetic recipe?